Understanding Risk Management and Hedging in Oil Trading

Chris Heilpern

Understanding Risk Management and Hedging in Oil Trading

A Practitioner's Guide to Managing Risk

palgrave
macmillan

Chris Heilpern
Nice, France

ISBN 978-3-031-44464-7   ISBN 978-3-031-44465-4 (eBook)
https://doi.org/10.1007/978-3-031-44465-4

© The Editor(s) (if applicable) and The Author(s), under exclusive license to Springer Nature Switzerland AG 2023

This work is subject to copyright. All rights are solely and exclusively licensed by the Publisher, whether the whole or part of the material is concerned, specifically the rights of translation, reprinting, reuse of illustrations, recitation, broadcasting, reproduction on microfilms or in any other physical way, and transmission or information storage and retrieval, electronic adaptation, computer software, or by similar or dissimilar methodology now known or hereafter developed.
The use of general descriptive names, registered names, trademarks, service marks, etc. in this publication does not imply, even in the absence of a specific statement, that such names are exempt from the relevant protective laws and regulations and therefore free for general use.
The publisher, the authors, and the editors are safe to assume that the advice and information in this book are believed to be true and accurate at the date of publication. Neither the publisher nor the authors or the editors give a warranty, expressed or implied, with respect to the material contained herein or for any errors or omissions that may have been made. The publisher remains neutral with regard to jurisdictional claims in published maps and institutional affiliations.

Cover illustration: Jan Engel/shutterstock

This Palgrave Macmillan imprint is published by the registered company Springer Nature Switzerland AG
The registered company address is: Gewerbestrasse 11, 6330 Cham, Switzerland

Paper in this product is recyclable.

Acknowledgments

The proximate cause of my writing this book is my friend Adi Imsirovic's book on trading and pricing crude oil. Adi's writing, encouragement, and suggestions were a great help and pushed me to not only write this book but also to make an effort to organize it and make it look professional. Deeper inspirations come from Suzanne Taylor, a colleague and a long-time friend, who was instrumental and essential in launching my career in teaching and training. I am deeply grateful to her for entrusting me with her work and her legacy. Special mention goes to Tarek Amyuni, the Director of the Masters Program in Financial Markets at SKEMA Business School, who hired me to teach commodity trading and turned me loose for ten years on unsuspecting students. And of course, I thank my colleagues at CITAC and IBH who have put up with me over the past decade and sent me around the world to teach oil markets and trading. Thanks to John Driscoll who made countless corrections and suggestions. Also Cyrille Costes who gave me some wise advice and tamed some of my less reasonable writing instincts. I also greatly appreciate the input, assistance, and extreme patience shown by solicitors, barristers, and in-house counsels who have hired me as an expert for various trading disputes. I learned as much about law and markets from them as I gave back in my expert opinions. I also bizarrely thank Sars-Cov-19 for closing down the world and forcing me to sit down in front of my computer and start writing this. Finally, I thank my wife Séverine who put up with me during my years of research for this book, which is to say, when I was working and living the not-always-pure or reasonable life of an oil trader for twenty years.

Contents

1	**Introduction**	1
2	**What Is Risk?**	3
3	**Some, but Not All, of the Risks in Trading**	9
	3.1 Price Risk	9
	3.2 Operational Risk	10
	3.3 Contractual Risk	12
	3.4 Legal Risk	16
	3.5 Payment Risk	17
	3.6 Personal Risk	19
4	**Managing Risk**	23
	4.1 Operational Risk	23
	4.2 Contractual Risk	27
	4.3 Legal Risk	32
	4.4 Payment Risk	42
	4.5 Personal Risk	45
5	**Price Risk**	49
	5.1 What is Price Risk?	52
	5.2 One Notion of "Long"	53
	5.3 One Notion of "Short"	53
	5.4 Long Price Positions	54
	5.5 Short Price Positions	57
	5.6 Short and Long with Floating Price Contracts	59

Contents

6	**Hedging Price Risk**		**79**
	6.1 What is a Hedge?		79
	6.2 Basic Principles of Hedging		80
	6.3 Imperfect Hedging or Basis Risk		84
7	**Using Basis Risk as a Trading Strategy**		**87**
	7.1 Examples of Basis Risk Hedging: Crude Oil Pricing		87
	7.2 Basis Risk and Hedging: Shipping Diesel from Asia to Europe		89
	7.3 A Quick Summary of Risk and Hedging		92
8	**Basic Derivatives**		**95**
	8.1 Swaps		95
	8.2 Cleared Swaps, Futures Exchanges, and Counterparty Risk		101
	8.3 Some Problems with Swaps		102
	8.4 Brent vs. Dubai Spread Risk: Another Look		104
9	**Futures Contracts and Forward Contracts**		**113**
	9.1 The Basics of Futures Contracts		113
	9.2 Hedging Physical Oil with Futures: US Crude and WTI Futures		117
	9.3 How are Futures and Swaps Different When Used to Hedge?		119
	9.4 Where Do the Prices of Futures Come From? What Do They Mean?		121
	9.5 Elephants and Bottles of Water: Explaining Contango and Backwardation		123
	9.6 The Forward Curve		126
	9.7 Do Contango and Backwardation Make Predictions About Prices?		129
	9.8 Forwards or Forward Contracts		131
	What are Forward Contracts?		131
10	**Options**		**133**
	10.1 What is an Option? A Simplified, Friendly Approach		133
	10.2 Calls and Puts		134
	10.3 "Half a Swap": Hedging with Options		136
	10.4 Average Price Options: Asian Calls or Caps		137
	10.5 Option Pricing…Simplified		139
11	**Hedging and Portfolio Risk**		**143**
	11.1 How do Traders Really Manage Price Risk?		143

12 Conclusion	149
Appendices	151
Bibliography	161
Index	163

List of Figures

Fig. 9.1	Simple graph of the forward curve of futures prices with just the price plots	127
Fig. 9.2	Forward curve as a line graph	127
Fig. 9.3	How our brain sees a forward curve	128
Fig. 9.4	Forward curve of a backwardated market	129

List of Tables

Table 5.1	Example of Platts prices and final contract price for a floating price fuel oil deal	72
Table 5.2	Creating a long position with average pricing over five days	73
Table 5.3	Building a position over a five day average pricing for 50,000 mt of fuel oil	74
Table 5.4	Five day average pricing table at the end of the first pricing day	75
Table 5.5	Five day average pricing table at the end of the last pricing day	76
Table 8.1	Analysis of prices for a sale of crude into Asia	105
Table 8.2	Prices for Dated Brent and Dubai for arbitrage trade	106
Table 8.3	P&L of crude oil arbitrage deal including hedging	108
Table 8.4	Table of prices and P&L for crude deal into West Africa	109
Table 8.5	Daily positions and change in positions on crude oil arbitrage deal into Asia	111
Table 9.1	Example of futures market screen with bid and offer for crude oil futures	114
Table 9.2	Example of physical and hedging positions for a crude oil cargo	120
Table 9.3	Example of futures list of prices	126
Table 9.4	Price list of forward curve of futures prices	128

1

Introduction

Books on hedging and risk all seem to be written by experts who have never bothered to explain those things to someone who did not already understand them. This could be because they cannot imagine that someone could not understand even the basics, such as what "being long" means. The explanations they give use examples and vocabulary which are nearly impenetrable to anyone who doesn't already understand risk and hedging. For example, a typical definition of a swap one finds in both academic and practical texts reads something like this: a swap is an exchange of a fixed income stream for a floating income stream. If you know what a swap is and how it works, you might understand that definition. Otherwise, I am pretty sure it leaves the uninitiated entirely in the dark. This book is an attempt to demystify and explain risk and hedging in simple terms.

I have traded physical oil "in the old days" when we did not hedge, mostly because we did not understand it and the markets we operated in were not developed enough to cover our risks. I have also traded in sophisticated, deep, and liquid markets where physical and derivative positions were interwoven for both hedging and speculation. Finally, I worked at investment banks where I provided hedging to clients and managed the risk those positions created in my own book. All through my career I met traders who used swaps, options, and futures without entirely understanding how they worked or what their risk really was. In fact, I cannot recall any formal training in

Supplementary Information The online version contains a free hedging workbook with detailed answers available at https://doi.org/10.1007/978-3-031-44465-4_1.

derivatives during my years at an oil major, trading company, or investment bank. Traders were supposed to learn on the go or it was assumed they knew everything already. Any misconceptions or uncertainties they had were never cleared up; for the most part, this imperfect understanding was not a problem and the traders managed their positions without catastrophes, at least not catastrophes linked to their hedging.

Having taught oil trading and risk management for over twelve years now, I can confidently say that ninety-five percent of the people I have taught have not really understood risk and hedging before joining my courses.[1] This ranges from physical traders who never used derivatives before to purely derivative traders who bought and sold hundreds of millions of barrels of futures without understanding what the prices really mean and who had no idea how those prices were created. And yet, understanding risk and hedging is easy if approached in a clear and simple fashion.

This book will try to explain risk and hedging in the simplest manner I can construct without reducing oil trading to a third grade level. The only math skills required to trade oil and hedge the risk are addition, subtraction, multiplication, and division. There are very few, if any, complex calculations in simple hedging. Of course, if you want to go beyond simple derivatives into the world of options, you might confront the dreaded Black–Scholes Formula, Monte Carlo Simulations, Volatility Surfaces, and Heteroskedasticity, but rest assured, you won't encounter them here.

If you are interested in working out more examples of price risk and hedging after you have read this book, you can try the exercises in the accompanying hedging and risk workbook (available as a download on the book's page on Chapter 1). The exercises run from simple to complex including floating price deals and contango hedging; complete answers with in-depth explanations are provided in the answer book.

---

[1] This might seem obvious, but I teach both introductory and advanced courses on risk and hedging. I am wise enough to not even take a guess at how many understood those things *after* taking my courses. As with many fields, learning to trade oil and manage risk cannot be done by taking a five day course. It requires that plus on the job training and experience. And, of course, buying and reading this book.

2

What Is Risk?

Risk is about losing money (ignoring for now the legal, moral, and health risks generally associated with oil trading). Most deals and positions are binary, which is to say there are two possible outcomes: they lose money or they make money. You can consider "breaking even" as being either zero losses or zero profits. Every deal has risk, even those we call "risk-free" or "back-to-back." In fact, the primary role of a trader is not, as some suppose, to manage risk, but to create it. Yes, his job is to make money, but that is the role of everyone who works for a living: you contribute in some way to the bottom line by adding to it or preventing it from dropping. There is no such thing as a free lunch in business. If a trader wants to make money, he has to do a deal. Every deal carries some risk, and the greater the risk, the greater the reward…at least, in theory.

What about those "back-to-back" deals I mentioned? Surely those are risk-free, right? Let's define a back-to-back deal and give an example. A back-to-back deal is a transaction in which the terms and conditions of the purchase match almost exactly the terms and conditions of the sale; any contractual terms the trader has with his supplier can be applied to the trader's receiver. An example is buying a standard cargo of physical oil on the market and reselling it.[1]

A trader buys a cargo of 30,000 metric tonnes of jet fuel from a major oil company, MajorCo, loading during the first week of the following month

---

[1] For those of you who have little to no experience in oil markets, you might need to consult the glossary in the appendix. The quality and characteristics of the vessel, the jet fuel, refinery, etc., are unimportant for this example and most of the others. Suffice to say that jet fuel is an oil product used by airlines to make their planes fly.

and agrees to a fixed price of $600 per metric tonne; the terms of the contract are standard (though this doesn't really matter as long as the purchase and sale contracts have the same terms). The trader then resells that same cargo to an airline, FlightCo, at $605 per metric tonne (MT); the sales contract is identical to the purchase contract except for the names of the buyer and seller and the price. Under most legal frameworks, including English law, we would expect the contract to apply to both deals in the same way. If the payment clause states that payment is to be made five days after the vessel has loaded, then the trader must pay MajorCo five days after loading and FlightCo must pay the trader five days after loading. The trader pays for the jet fuel and receives money for the jet fuel on the same day. This concept should apply to all the clauses of the contracts, assuming they are identical.

So why isn't this deal risk-free? How could the trader lose money? Surely, the five dollar margin is as good as in the bank as soon as he concludes both deals. Sadly, this is not the case, though many traders assume it is. If it were, if risk-free trades existed, there would be traders or even algorithms (computer programs) which executed those deals with ever-declining margins; theoretically, the margin or price difference between the purchase and sale contracts would be reduced to some small but "reasonable" level just above transaction costs (brokerage fees, operations, inspection fees, paperwork, IT costs, etc.). So why isn't this the case?

The two contracts are called "back-to-back," but it is clear that they are not identical. They differ in two important ways: the counterparties and the prices. These two terms of the contract are not minor details. If MajorCo fails to perform the contract, what can the trader do? He certainly cannot simply tell FlightCo, his buyer, "Tough luck! No jet fuel for you!" The trader still has an obligation to perform the sales contract. If MajorCo fails to deliver and the market for Jet Fuel is now at $670 per MT, the trader must buy a cargo at that price and deliver it to FlightCo for $605. It is not at all certain that he can hold MajorCo responsible for all the costs and consequences. Imagine that the deal to FlightCo was for a delivery into Rotterdam. The purchase from MajorCo was from a port in North West Europe. A sale for delivery of a 30,000 metric tonne cargo of Jet Fuel into Rotterdam is a very liquid contract which could be fulfilled from almost any refinery in the world. MajorCo declares Force Majeure and informs the trader that they will not be delivering a cargo of Jet Fuel to them. It is not at all certain that the trader can declare Force Majeure as well unless the cause of the Force Majeure is general to the market and not specific to MajorCo's refinery or port. For example, if MajorCo's only European refinery blew up, this might be acceptable as a case of Force Majeure for MajorCo, but it would be unlikely to apply to the trader since he could buy Jet Fuel from anywhere and anyone else to perform his contract with FlightCo.

Alternatively, suppose FlightCo declared bankruptcy after signing the deal. While FlightCo is still legally bound by the contract, it doesn't mean they will perform it, can perform it, or will be able to pay for the oil. In fact, the trader might decide that FlightCo's bankruptcy entitles him to cancel the contract. I am sure that the trader's finance department would not be happy with delivering $18 million worth of Jet to a company that has just declared that it has no money to pay for it. In this case, the trader might end up selling the jet fuel at a distressed price. Even worse, FlightCo might declare bankruptcy after receiving the cargo but prior to making payment. Any trader who has been in the market long enough has faced losses related to bankruptcies; I lost a few tens of thousands on trades I had with Enron when they went from being the darling of Wall Street to being a bankrupt Ponzi scheme.

In the first case, MajorCo declaring Force Majeure, we would expect the trader to seek redress and compensation from MajorCo. Unfortunately, there is no guaranty that the court or the arbitration board will rule in favor of the trader; they could uphold MajorCo's declaration of Force Majeure. If the trader had in turn declared Force Majeure (he passed it on) to FlightCo, a different court or arbitration board could determine that the trader was not entitled to declare Force Majeure. This might be unusual and rare but has happened, at least according to legal experts I have consulted in London. While a court decision in favor of MajorCo (i.e., the court upholds the Force Majeure) might imply that another judge would most likely uphold the trader's declaration of Force Majeure to FlightCo, there is no guaranty of this. The court decision in Trader v. MajorCo relates only to the contract between the trader and MajorCo, not the contract between the trader and FlightCo, though the first court decision creates a precedent and jurisprudence. Arbitration is generally private and confidential, though, so a different set of arbitrators would not be able to rely on the earlier decision. Back-to-back contracts are separate legal documents subject to different interpretations and different results.

There might also be marketing considerations when contemplating passing through the enforcement of terms and conditions from the seller to the buyer. If MajorCo commits a breach of contract such as under-loading the cargo (not meeting the contractual minimum quantity), arriving late or failing to provide proper documentation in a timely fashion, the trader might not want to make a claim against MajorCo and then pass on the costs and consequences to FlightCo. He might instead value the commercial relationship with both companies to such a degree that he feels obligated to compensate FlightCo without making claims against MajorCo. This is relative, though, since most traders would make claims against the supplier and try to avoid compensating the buyer when the amounts involved were hundreds of thousands or millions of dollars.

These examples show that back-to-back physical contracts are not risk-free. There is always a chance that something will go wrong in a deal and the trader in the middle may decide that he does not want to try to recover costs that he has incurred for fear of damaging a commercial relationship. Take the case of an oil company with a contract with a national oil ministry for buying straight run fuel oil from their refinery. For one of the liftings the ministry informed the company that they would not give the contractual quantity that had been nominated but would instead deliver the minimum allowed under the contract.

This was a clear breach of contract. The cargo was 80,000 metric tonnes with a tolerance of ten percent in the buyer's option (the oil company could choose to load between 72,000 and 88,000 metric tonnes). The oil company had resold the cargo and the option on the loading quantity to a large and well-known trading house that had nominated the full contractual volume of 88,000 metric tonnes. The refinery provided only 72,000 metric tonnes, a shortfall of 16,000 metric tonnes versus the nominated quantity. The cargo was heading to the US with a freight cost of over twenty dollars per tonne. In addition, the cargo was profitable. In all, the trader was going to make $400,000 less than he could reasonably expect if the full cargo had been loaded. The trader made a claim against the oil company. The oil company did not pass on the claim to national oil company because of their long and deep relationship with the ministry of energy; the oil company had equity production of crude oil, a long-standing refining agreement, traditional access to the crude oil and products contracts, and plans in place for natural gas projects. All of this was worth hundreds of billions and the oil company would not risk it for a small claim. Despite the short loading claim being valid, the trading house also dropped their claim and accepted a nice lunch instead of the $400,000, leading me to believe they valued their commercial relationship with the oil company at much higher than $400,000.

Some might say that, yes, there is a risk-free trade. Trading futures on the major exchanges are, they say, risk-free. I would agree that out of all the deals a trader can do in the oil markets, buying and selling futures on ICE or the CME is about as close to risk-free as you can get assuming you ignore the fundamental element of what a futures contract is. A futures contract is a fixed price trade which instantly creates a price risk.[2] There is no such thing as a back-to-back trade on futures since you cannot re-trade them to a third party; you buy and sell from the exchange at different times even if those times are milliseconds apart. And even if we ignore price risk, there is a small but real possibility of the exchange declaring bankruptcy or otherwise disappearing (a hack of the entire ICE system and all the backup servers would wipe out all legal evidence of trades), your computer terminal breaking or an international internet cable being severed. These events might sound highly improbable to you, but I spent a few days trading in Singapore without internet and very limited phone connections when a trans-Pacific cable was cut; we had to call our offices in New York and London to make trades on the futures markets.

If back-to-back trades with identical terms and conditions are not risk-free, then this implies that risk increases the more we change the two contracts and make them less and less alike. The smaller the difference the less risk it creates, but every difference increases risk. If we buy a cargo FOB under English law with disputes settled by the High Court in London and then resell that cargo back-to-back to another company under Chinese Law with the arbitration in Beijing, there is no guaranty that any sort of dispute or claim will be adjudicated in the same manner in each of those places. That is to say, in the event of a breach of contract, the trader might sue the FOB seller and in turn get sued by the company he sold to under the back-to-back contract. The High Court of London could rule in favor of the original FOB seller and make the trader pay all the legal fees and court costs, which can amount to millions of dollars in a large case. The trader could then lose his case in Beijing and be forced to pay his receiver millions in compensation for the breach as well as his legal fees for the proceedings. While it is true that only a small portion of trades end up in disputes and a small portion of those end up in court (or arbitration), the costs and risks can be very high. Simply believing that the risk of losing both cases is so low as to be non-existent is to ignore the realities of trading disputes and the sometimes inexplicable reasoning of both judges and arbitrators.

Each difference between the contracts or positions creates additional risk. Some have a low probability of causing a problem, as in the case of legal jurisdiction, but have a high cost associated with that risk. Other differences in the terms and conditions have a high probability of causing a loss but may have a low cost associated with that risk. For example, the demurrage rate in the two contracts might differ by $100 per day. The odds of incurring

---

[2] More on this later. Basically you buy a contract at, say, $100 per barrel which is a "fixed price." If the market goes down, your contract is worth less and you lose money when you resell it. If the market goes up, you make money. That is pretty much the definition of risk.

demurrage on any given physical deal are high so we can expect the trader to lose money. In this case, if we assume that all the parties agree to the calculations of laytime and demurrage and pay the demurrage (the FOB seller pays the trader and the trader pays his FOB[3] buyer), then the trader stands to lose at most $100 per day of demurrage. In even an extreme case of one hundred days of demurrage, this would amount to a trifling $10,000. It is, nonetheless, a risk.

If there are no risk-free trades, how does a trader make money? The answer is that traders enter into deals which have a lower risk than reward (or conversely, the reward is greater than the risk). So a trader might enter into a deal where he judges that he could reasonably lose one dollar and reasonably expect to earn ten dollars. Additionally, traders manage their risk in order to minimize losses. This is not quite the same as making a back-to-back deal. Instead, managing risk is about dealing with risk that has been incurred when the risky position or trade was created. This amounts to understanding how all the aspects of trading work and having competent, proactive people managing the trades. Let's break out our risks into a short, but non-exhaustive, list.

Once I have explained the various risks, I will present brief sections on how to manage each of those risks. The final section, and the main subject of this book, will be about price risk and hedging. I believe that it is important for anyone entering the oil market to understand that simply because his price risk is hedged does not mean he doesn't have risk. While it is true that the greatest losses in commodity trading came about from poorly managed price risk, there have been billions lost on these other risks as well.

---

[3] FOB means "Free On Board." It is an Incoterm (International Commercial Term) which means the buyer of the cargo has to show up with a vessel and load the cargo from the seller. Other Incoterms are defined in the appendix.

3

Some, but Not All, of the Risks in Trading

I usually tell my students that anything that can go wrong, will go wrong, or has already gone wrong for me personally in my career. I have experienced theft, piracy, mutinies, pollution spills, contaminations, delays, Force Majeure, fraud, bankruptcy, and incompetence to list just a few. A trader can't go through life continuously thumbing through The Black Swan[1] and surrounded by a phalanx of lawyers because of all that. But a little preparation and understanding of what can or might happen goes a long way. Here are some, but not all, of the risks you might encounter when trading oil.

3.1 Price Risk

The main goal of this book is to talk about hedging price risk so I will address that at length later. It is sufficient to say for now that prices go up and down and those movements can cause losses. If a trader buys one million barrels of oil at 75 US dollars per barrel, he hopes the market will rise so he can sell higher and make a profit. If the market drops to 70 US dollars per barrel, the trader loses five million dollars. So price risk is the possibility of losing money because oil prices move around, go up and down, or, as we say in the industry, float. More on this later. If you are impatient to learn about price risk, jump ahead to Chapter 5, but be sure to come back to Chapter 3 later on. The other risks are as important.

---

[1] Nassim Taleb's book explains how the greatest risks you face are those you cannot even imagine as possible to begin with.

3.2 Operational Risk

Operational risk is the possibility of losing money because something breaks down. This could be mechanical such as a pipe bursting or a ship sinking. It could be procedural such as forgetting to send an invoice or missing a time bar (time limit for filing a claim). Sometimes operational risk is nobody's fault. For example, if a storm sinks your oil tanker, that is Force Majeure. Whether or not someone is at fault or if was just bad luck, breakdowns in operations can lead to real losses, sometimes severe losses.

Operational risks include demurrage, contaminations, delays, losses, and errors in blending and delivery timing. Traders tend to be natural risk seekers (either by personality or by the nature of the business) who will test the limits of their contractual responsibilities. For example, a trader who has a commitment to deliver a cargo by 25th of the month might delay making a purchase to cover that commitment in hopes of finding a cheap cargo or a distressed seller. This might mean he misses his contractual delivery dates. In most cases this is not catastrophic for anyone, assuming the delay is minor. The delay might, however, lead to unrecoverable demurrage for the trader or even penalties for late delivery.

Losses and contaminations generally result from choosing poor infrastructure such as a cheap vessel or making risky decisions on loading certain qualities on board vessels which are not entirely suitable to carry those qualities (e.g., loading diesel on a vessel which previously carried heavy fuel oil and hoping it was cleaned well enough to avoid contamination). Losses can result from buying from unreliable sources or performing ship to ship transfers (or worse, multiple ship to ship transfers) with invoiced quantities measured at the point of delivery (i.e., in the ultimate shore tanks after discharge). Traders can also accept inadequate guarantees or accept inappropriate testing and measuring methods. This can lead to losses and off-specification cargoes.

Delays are inevitable in trading. This principle is even entrenched in shipping contracts (charter parties[2]) and maritime law where shipowners are generally not held responsible for arriving late for a loading (hence the term "laycan" which means "laydays or canceling," essentially meaning that the shipowner will do his best to perform the agreed dates but can't be penalized for being late beyond having the contract canceled). Ships are often victims of weather and port congestion. The Ever Given blocked the Suez Canal for a week which blocked and delayed hundreds of oil tankers on laden and ballast

---

[2] A charter party is the contract between the shipowner and someone who needs a vessel to transport oil. It is separate from the contract to buy and sell the oil; that contract is usually called the commercial contract.

voyages.[3] Delays can be caused by the failures of suppliers and buyers alike. A supplier might be late in preparing the cargo or the trader might be unable to arrange his financing for a week or more. In these cases, the vessel is delayed in arriving at discharge, arriving at load port or loading the cargo. All of these things are beyond the control of shipowners; the industry and the law do not hold them responsible for these events.

This notion of "stuff happens" does not generally extend to commercial contracts. Suppliers and traders can be and are held responsible for late deliveries, sometimes with severe penalties and costs. If we take the case of a delivery of crude oil which arrives very late, it might lead to the refinery shutting down; this could lead to costs and claims in the tens of millions of dollars. It is not acceptable for the trader to deny responsibility by saying his vessel was late. There are exceptions to this principle which fall under what is called Force Majeure. Without going into legal details, Force Majeure can be considered Acts of God which are outside the control of the party affected as well as being unpredictable. An earthquake that destroys a refinery might prevent the refiner (or a trader who bought an FOB cargo from that refiner) from performing the contract; the buyer of the oil is unlikely to have any recourse since this would likely be a case of Force Majeure. The buyer would need to find an alternative cargo and suffer any extra costs that follow.

Operational risks are managed in two main stages. First, the trader enters into deals which are feasible and manageable. By feasible we mean that, all going well, the deal can be performed according to its contractual terms and conditions. By manageable, we mean that the operations are within the knowledge and experience of the trading company. As an example of an unfeasible and unmanageable deal, we could imagine an oil trader entering into a CIF[4] delivery of one hundred and fifty thousand tonnes of sugar beets for delivery to San Francisco in seven days. It seems unlikely that such a large cargo could be found at all let alone loaded and delivered to the US West Coast in only seven days. It is further highly unlikely that the operators at an oil trading company know how beets are handled, what documents are required, or what kind of ship is needed (I chose beets because I know

---

[3] A laden voyage means the vessel is carrying cargo. A ballast voyage means it has no cargo and is returning empty except perhaps for ballast water.

[4] CIF is another Incoterm which means "Cost, Insurance, Freight." If you sell a cargo CIF, you are delivering it to your buyer and the price includes shipping and insurance. I tend to use CIF (or "siff" as we often pronounce it) as a short-hand for any type of delivered contract since it is quicker to say "siff" than say "delivered." Traders are often lazy this way and use abbreviations or shortened expressions. Crude oil traders, for example, trade the price difference between CME NYMEX Light Sweet Crude futures and ICE Brent Crude futures. This "spread" is called the "Brent-TI." Brent is obvious but "TI" means WTI (West Texas Intermediate crude oil) which is the main crude delivered under the NYMEX contract. Pronouncing the letter "w" requires three extra syllables so it's dropped!

nothing about beet trading. According to some quick internet research, total global sugar beet exports are about five hundred thousand tonnes per year, so a cargo of 150,000 mt seems preposterous and frankly impossible).

The second stage of managing operational risk is to have competent, motivated, and experienced back office staff. It is possible to run a small trading office with two or three people (e.g., two traders and an operator), but they would be quickly overwhelmed by any big problem that arose.

3.3 Contractual Risk

When a contract is agreed, it binds the trader to do or accept certain things. If a trader agrees to deliver ten million barrels of Bonny Light crude oil to China at $1 per barrel, he has entered into a binding deal which will cost him hundreds of millions of dollars (at least at today's market prices of around 80 dollars per barrel). If a trader commits to lift sixty thousand tonnes of jet fuel every month for a year from Abu Dhabi, the trader will have to dispose of that jet fuel on the market in some fashion. The first step in creating risk is entering into a deal. If the deal is misunderstood or incomplete, additional risk is created.

Every clause of a contract is binding.[5] Every word counts. Often in our everyday lives, we sign or accept contracts without reading them or understanding them because we are too busy to do so or we simply can't work out the legalese. We are often told that the contract is "standard" or "boiler plate" and "everyone accepts it." This might be true, but that doesn't mean you should not read it first. While I doubt you can get the desk agent at a car rental company to change the clauses of the standard rental agreement, you can always try to negotiate any contract including most contracts in the oil markets. If there is a clause in the car rental agreement you truly don't like, try crossing it out, initialing that spot, and passing it back to the agent; the odds are good the agent won't bother checking what you deleted or added and will process the contract with your amendments! That new contract is binding! Don't believe me? Look up the story about a man who bamboozled a bank by signing up for a credit card with free, unlimited credit (Dmitry Agarkov and Tinkoff Credit Systems).[6]

---

[5] This is not strictly true. A clause which requires that a party commit an illegal activity would not be binding. Under English law a contract cannot amend or change certain characteristics of a bill of lading.

[6] Agarkov rewrote a standard credit card application he received in the mail and returned it to the bank. They processed the application without reading it and issued him a credit card with zero interest and heavy penalties to be paid to Agarkov if the bank canceled the card. The court decided

Contracts do not need to be written or final to be binding. A handshake, a nod, or a "yes" can all lead to binding contracts. It is sometimes the case in trading, at least for many physical contracts, that the physical delivery is undertaken and often completed before the written contract is finalized (this is becoming less common as most companies install back office systems which generate and transmit contracts almost immediately). This is generally caused by the legal departments of the buyer and seller arguing over the use of a comma or a semi-colon in an obscure sub-clause. In an ideal world, the traders concluding the deal would negotiate and agree to every clause of the contract down to the grammar and spelling. In reality, this does not often happen.

There are many reasons why traders don't go over every detail of the contract when they conclude a deal. Most traders assume that the key elements matter while the rest of the terms are just "lawyer stuff." These traders will be sure to negotiate the quality, the quantity, the price, the delivery dates, the payment terms, and the demurrage rates but will gloss over or simply ignore terms such as jurisdiction, limitation of liability, suitability, Force Majeure, etc. This is often a reasonable attitude to take when dealing with a familiar counterparty with whom the trader does frequent, consistent, and similar trades. The traders operate under the assumption that the other undiscussed terms and conditions will be as per usual, as per the last deal, or as per usual industry terms and conditions.

It sometimes happens that traders are unhappy with their deal and try to get out of it by claiming that it was not contractually binding since many of the terms and conditions had not been discussed (i.e., all the boring bits that only the lawyers read were not specifically agreed to during the negotiations). For the most part, judges and arbitrators take a dim view of this stance and generally tell the trader that if they were intending to deviate from their usual terms (between the two companies or what would pass for standard terms and conditions on the market) they should have raised those deviations as part of the negotiations in the same manner they discussed prices and quantities, for example. It is indeed sufficient to tell a broker or a counterparty "done" with almost no details being discussed in order for a contract to be binding. This would clearly be the case in a highly standardized market like Brent Forwards (BFOET paper). If a trader offered to sell a September Brent at $78.25 to another trader who responded with "Done," it is clear to everyone, including judges, that the parties entered into a full contract with specific and agreed

---

that the bank sent out an offer which Agarkov countered with his own terms. The bank accepted the new terms. The bank argued in court that they had not read the contract and should not be held to it! The bank lost the case.

terms and conditions for the delivery of 600,000 barrels of North Sea crude oil during the month of September. It is hopeless for the trader to try to hide behind an argument like "we did not specify the quantity" since the quantity is specified by the very definition of what a Brent Forward contract is.

Sometimes traders avoid discussing certain terms and conditions altogether. A trader might assume that he is going to get a specific condition in the contract and simply doesn't bother bringing it up. This could be something with little impact on the deal such as his preferred wording for the Force Majeure clause or it could be something that the other trader might not want to accept such as arbitration in Beijing instead of arbitration in London. Both clauses depend on unlikely events such as Force Majeure or a contractual dispute that cannot be resolved amicably. In the case of the Force Majeure clause, there is a low likelihood that the preferred wording is truly unacceptable to the market and therefore would not lead to the deal being broken. For the arbitration clause, it is entirely plausible and likely that a company would refuse to accept arbitration in Beijing for an international oil contract with English law; the trader's legal department might categorically refuse such a clause whatever the trader might say.

Sometimes the trader avoids mentioning terms or conditions in the hope of not having to make a contractual commitment. For example, a trader can sell a cargo of a heavy fuel oil blending component (a product which does not generally have official specifications so the quality needs to be fully discussed during the negotiation. This is contrary to jet fuel where technically you don't have to do more than call it "Jet A-1" since official, international aviation specifications exist which tell you exactly what Jet A-1 must look like.). If the seller is aware that one of the specifications of his product is difficult to deal with or presents a cost to any buyer, he may choose to ignore this specification during negotiations since bringing it up will lower the value of the cargo or even break the deal. If the buyer never bothers to specify his requirements or desired specifications but simply assumes the fuel oil will look like typical fuel oil in the market, he might find himself with a product that is worth far less than he thought. It is no good coming back after the cargo has been loaded and the quality measured to complain that "the CCR[7] is very high and should be no more than 18 since everyone knows that is the limit for the market, etc." It is too late at that point. If this example seems fairly specific, it is because it happened to me. I sold a cargo which I knew would have a

---

[7] CCR is Conradsen Carbon Residue. This specification measures how much coke and residue is left after a fuel is burned. When you burn wood in a fire, it produces ash. Ideally, you want all your wood to turn into heat, light, and smoke. Too much ash means lots of wood that did not do its job. CCR is the equivalent for oil, so a lower CCR (less leftover cinders) is better than a higher CCR.

very high CCR. I never brought it up, and when the buyer started talking about specifications, I quickly changed the subject. This cost the buyer quite a bit of money, but he never held it against me since it was clearly his fault for not bringing it up during the negotiations.

Sometimes a trader will go even further and include terms and conditions which were not discussed but which have a material and definite impact on the deal. For example, a trader might insert, buried deep in the boring legal clauses, a clause which extends an annual term contract automatically unless canceled by the buyer. Or a clause which modifies the price; again, this clause would be hidden somewhere other than in the paragraph entitled "Price Clause." Is this moral? That is the wrong question to be asking in the world of oil trading. Is this legal? Certainly. When a company accepts a contract, there is a strong legal assumption that they read the contract. It is farcical for a major oil company like BP or a top oil trader like Mercuria to claim they were naive and taken advantage of because they did not read or understand the contract.

A final word on contractual risk and the contract. The contract is not, despite what it might say at the very end, "final and binding." It is certainly binding, but is not necessarily final. Under English law, there are ways to change the contract without the explicit written consent of the other party. This is covered by the Basic Rule and Deviation (or breach of contract). In the case where one party deviates from the contract and informs the other party of the breach, if the non-breaching party does not object, complain, or declare that there has been a breach, then it is tantamount to accepting that the contract has been modified. For example, a trader has contracted to deliver a minimum of 30,000 MT of gasoline to a buyer but then notifies the buyer prior to loading the cargo that he will load only 29,000 MT. If the buyer carries on without reacting, simply acknowledging the loading as usual, nominating a joint inspector, and ultimately accepting the cargo at discharge, it is assumed under English law that the buyer was perfectly happy to modify the contract and change the minimum quantity to 29,000 MT. It would be unacceptable for the buyer to take delivery and then suddenly make a claim for a breach. This principle of "He who doesn't protest, accepts" is why the legal and operations departments spend so much ink on messages going back and forth notifying the counterparty that whatever they did was unacceptable and all costs and consequences are for them every time there is the slightest deviation from the contract.

3.4 Legal Risk

One needs only type "oil trading scandal" into any search engine to come up with a long list of stories of bribery, theft, cheating, lying, collusion, drunkenness, and debauchery in the oil industry. Traders come back from long lunches and drunkenly buy fifty million barrels of futures (interestingly enough, we only hear about these drunken trades when they lose money). Traders get caught manipulating markets and sometimes get banned or pay fines. Bribes are also common in oil trading, with amounts ranging from a few hundred dollars for lunch to billions paid over decades. Most companies immediately blame a few bad apples and declare that the company is clean, honest, and fair. Sadly, this does not really appear to be the case.

Lying, bribing, and manipulating are part and parcel of the oil industry for almost all aspects of the business, trading above all. For the most part the costs (penalties and fines) associated with these activities have been small or moderate. If we look at the fines imposed on oil traders (by this I mean the company which employs the trader, and this could include oil majors or independent trading companies), they are small compared to the profits made from bribery. Much like the fines paid by Wall Street banks, they are just small costs of doing business. Recently a large trading company agreed to pay a few hundred million in fines for corruption in their South American dealing; during the same year that company earned billions in profits. Crime, or at least alleged crime, pays…very well. Other top trading firms have recorded huge profits over the past decade while seeing several of their top oil traders face civil and criminal charges. The same can be said for the trading departments at oil majors. This does not mean that all their business is corrupt, but that corruption and cheating are integral parts of the oil trading business.

While crime typically pays, it is not necessarily something oil companies want to be made public. These days most of the largest traders are listed companies or aspiring to go public or attract investors. There are real consequences for getting caught beyond the pesky fines and very occasional jail sentences for the individuals involved. The company mainly risks seeing its share price decline. This translates into large losses for the traders and managers who receive a significant part of their bonuses in shares. In reality, the market does not care about corruption in the medium or long term. As long as the company keeps making money and does not get caught too often or in a too sordid affair, the market is happy to keep working with them and buying their shares.

For the individual traders, the consequences of getting caught doing "business as usual" are more painful. Though the cases are rare, there have been heavy fines (millions of dollars) and jail terms for traders caught lying, cheating, bribing, and manipulating. The traders are often banned from the market, though it is not clear if they are banned from other markets and jurisdictions. So a trader who is caught in the US might be forbidden from working in the commodity or finance markets in the US but might get a job in Switzerland, London, or Singapore. It all depends on how much money he can bring in. For those who made tens or even hundreds of millions trading oil, a fine of a few million dollars is annoying but hardly lifestyle-changing. The traders in question probably end up paying as much in legal fees as fines.

As for prison sentences, they are rare, mainly because proving market manipulation is difficult. And even when it has been demonstrated, it is not clear that a judge or jury will understand how it all works anyway. The recent cases in the LIBOR markets in London show that getting caught red-handed doing something which is complicated and hard to explain probably means getting away with it. If, though, the trader is found guilty, courts have started taking a more dim view of these activities. What used to be a few clever boys exploiting the system and making a few bucks is now seen as what it really is: theft, bribery, cheating, lying, and manipulation. The penalties are getting harsher. A recent case in California oil trading has led to discussions of civil penalties (barred from the market and fines) as well as criminal penalties (prison, loss of nationality, and deportation). For the most part, the traders and the company admit no wrongdoing but agree to a fine and perhaps a ban for the trader. Again, this is because financial fraud and trading fraud are hard to prove to a jury.

3.5 Payment Risk

While demurrage, contamination, and fines can sometimes lead to tens or hundreds of millions in losses, the one risk that really focuses companies' attention is payment risk. When a trader sells a cargo of oil, he is handing over the oil to the buyer and hopes to receive money for the cargo. A cargo of two million barrels of crude oil is worth about 160 million US dollars, an amount which dwarfs "petty fines" or even hefty demurrage bills. Trading companies often have exposure to one counterparty (i.e., a buyer) for multiple cargoes worth half a billion dollars or more. When this exposure is added to risk from derivatives, mainly "Over-The-Counter" swaps and options, the risk can be multiplied a few times. Even Exxon or Shell would feel a pinch of pain if a client who owed them 750 million dollars went belly up (bankrupt).

Payment risk comes in many forms, the simplest being the risk of not getting paid on a specific physical transaction. The trader sells a cargo to a company, delivers the cargo, and then waits for payment. If no payment is forthcoming, the trader will usually have a hard time recovering the oil. If the payment was to be made thirty days after delivery, it is likely that the oil has already been consumed or resold; it cannot be seized. These kinds of problems are typically rare but not unheard of.

Another payment risk is delayed payment. Trading companies, especially smaller ones, rely on banking lines (revolving credit) to finance their activity. If a client pays late, this has repercussions for the availability of credit to do fresh deals. The trader might find himself unable to access the oil market since he cannot arrange for payment for a cargo. This was the case in the aftermath of the Financial Crisis in 2008–2009. A profitable arbitrage existed between Europe and Asia for heavy fuel oil (that is to say, fuel oil was cheap in Europe and could be shipped cheaply to Asia where it could be sold at a large profit). The arbitrage remained in place (stayed "open") and even grew bigger (wider). It turned out that traders were unable to buy oil in Europe because the banks would not give them financing, so oil kept piling up in Europe while Asian supply dropped lower and lower.[8]

Late payments obviously trigger interest costs but there could also be provisions in the credit facility whereby the amount of the credit is reduced based on the poor quality of the trader's clients. These days banks are reticent to finance oil trading for any but the largest companies. Small traders find themselves shut out of markets entirely as banks look at reputational risk and experience losses from fraud or poor management (the Hin Leong, Hontop, and Zenrock scandals in Singapore have led to a few banks announcing their withdrawal from commodity trade finance). So if a trader chooses a few bad clients and finds himself explaining to his bank why he needs an overdraft for a few weeks, he might find that the bank or the consortium contributing to his credit facility no longer wants his business. Since few, if any, trading companies have enough cash to self-finance their trading business, the trader would either have to reduce his trading dramatically or stop altogether.

---

[8] If oil is piling up in Europe, the price in that market will drop. If stocks of oil are running low in Asia, the price in that market will rise. Asia will rise relative to Europe. Logically, it makes more and more sense to buy cheap oil in Europe and ship it to Asia. But this only works if you can find cash or financing to buy the oil in the first place!

3.6 Personal Risk

I touched on personal risk when talking about legal risk and illegal activities. A trader can end up paying a fine or going to jail. For those who think that white-collar, college-educated oil traders go to country-club jails with tennis courts, swimming pools, and Michelin chefs, you would be disappointed when you got there. Yes, some prisons in the US are Club Med compared to San Quentin, Alcatraz, or Rikers Island, but only in comparison. White-collar prisons are still mostly traditional prisons with cells and fences. Even those with tennis courts and honor systems (no fences) are not filled with only middle-aged accountants and Wall Street CEOs. They also house drug lords and mobsters convicted of fraud, tax evasion, or other white-collar crimes. Perhaps there are even hard-core murderers who squealed on former accomplices in return for a shorter sentence in a country-club prison. These people are violent sociopaths who will beat, stab, or rape other inmates if given the opportunity or provocation.

Most other countries don't have white-collar facilities. Nick Leeson, who committed bank fraud in Singapore, spent four years in Changi Prison where he was locked up twenty-two hours a day in a cell with three to seven other inmates. An oil trader in New York was convicted of fraud (unsurprisingly, he was charged because he stole from his employer, Citibank, and not from his clients or the market) and sentenced to jail in a "country-club" white-collar Federal prison; when it was discovered he had a pilot's license he was transferred to a medium security state prison outside Miami filled with hard-core criminals (The Federal "country-club" prison was adjacent to an Air Force base so it was assumed he could break out of prison, steal an F-16 and bomb Citibank headquarters or something like that). In reality, few oil traders end up in jail. Instead, a few end up in a personal hell or discomfort of some other kind.

Trading commodities is a stressful job. The rewards can be high but they come with a price. Humans don't mind a bit of stress in life; it is motivational. Good stresses include boredom which motivates you to read a book, meet up with friends, or learn to play guitar. Hunger is a biological stress which motivates us to eat. Cold weather, rocky floors, and windy caves all motivated early man to build shelters with windows, insulation, fireplaces, memory foam mattresses, and game rooms. Stress pushes and pulls society forward. But the stress created by trading is the wrong kind of stress and it doesn't motivate per se. It is the result of risk-seeking activity, not the cause of it. This is not a paper on human biology and psychology and many papers in those fields discuss good and bad stress and their effects on the human body. Plenty of information on the affects of stress on the mind and body can be found in a few hours of internet searches. Let us just say that the stress from trading leads to both psychological and physiological problems including depression, alcoholism, memory loss, heart disease, and high blood pressure.

Some traders "wake up screaming" every day of the week. From Monday to Friday they scream because they have to put on their game face, struggle through their impostor syndrome (the feeling that everyone else in the room is smart and grown up while they are immature and incompetent), suppress their stress, and convince themselves and the market that they are smarter, quicker, and hungrier than everyone else. On weekends they still wake up screaming because now they have to negotiate the unfamiliar territory and relationships of their family; they never see their kids during the week and see only a bit more of their wives. They try to decompress and de-stress but a weekend is too short for that. And their positions are still waiting for them in the office. They both want the weekend to be as short and as long as possible as they are torn between needing to get back to their desks where they believe they can control their lives and wanting to run away from the never-ending stress and pressures of trading.

Traders sometimes burn out early. I knew quite a few traders in their thirties and forties who had heart attacks or severe high blood pressure. Some cope, or believe they are coping, by using drugs or by drinking too much. The market is not really "The Wolf of Wall Street"; oil trading has cleaned itself up quite a bit over the past decade or so. But intense pressure is a feature of trading, and that pressure leads to physical and psychological problems as well as what we might call "poor lifestyle choices."

Trading is almost purely about making money. I tell my students that if they want to have a fruitful "Take Your Child to Work Day" or see monuments to their achievements, they should become engineers, artists, or doctors. Some traders build great companies like Vitol, Mercuria, and Trafigura; most have a legacy that can be reduced to a profit and loss column. Certainly, there are some who become well-known beyond the narrow world of oil trading both for good and bad reasons. Marc Rich is well-known outside of oil circles, but few of the right-wing Americans who despise him could probably talk coherently about his career; they only know Clinton pardoned him. Andy Hall was once called "God" by the trading community, but I doubt that in twenty years his name will be found outside of a few articles in Forbes or footnotes in books about the history of the industry. Who among you recognizes the names Chen Jiulin, Marco Dunand, Olav

Refvik, Isabelle Ealet, or Lim Oon Kuin? If you do, you are definitely in the oil business and probably in trading.

If traders leave little behind, what do they take with them? Mostly money and health problems. Is money enough to justify the stresses of a career in trading? Which is to say, can money buy happiness? It is likely that many traders would scoff at the question and tell you that the point is simply to make more money: more than last year and more than anyone else. Possibly, but that tautology doesn't answer any questions; it just says making money is good because you are making money. A study by Harvard University in 2010 showed that happiness peaks at about $75,000 a year. After that point, new acquisitions bring more problems and stress but not more satisfaction. A more recent study by the Wharton School of Business has yielded a different result which shows that happiness increases with wealth; being richer makes you happier. But both studies concluded that mere wealth does not provide happiness. Happiness comes from being able to experience things rather than owning things. Working eighty to one hundred hours a week with just a few weeks of vacation a year might let you buy an apartment in Manhattan, a condo in Vail, a summer house in the Hamptons, and his and her Ferraris at all those places, but it probably won't make you happy. Instead, happiness comes from being able to experience enjoyable and exciting things with friends and family.

Trading can be exhilarating even if it is stressful. My career took me around the globe from Paris to London to Singapore. I traded just about every kind of product in markets from the Baltics to China and most places in between. My contacts included oil ministers, leaders of newly formed countries, top traders, and good friends I made along the way. My business travels took me south to Capetown, north to Finland, west to New York, and east to Japan. Business lunches and dinners were in the finest restaurants and featured expensive wines, Cuban cigars, and one hundred-year-old brandy. It paid for my house and many other fine things. So it would be hypocritical of me to tell aspiring traders to try a calmer, less stressful career just because of the particular risks in trading. But anyone going into a trading job, in oil or any other market, should go in with the full knowledge of what the job entails and what the risks are.

4

Managing Risk

In this section we will look at the risks we have defined and described and consider ways to reduce or eliminate those risks. There are no perfect solutions just as there are no perfect back-to-back contracts. Managing risk is about choosing techniques and solutions which reduce the risk to a point which is acceptable to the trader and his company. Sometimes the trader is unable or unwilling to manage his risk, in which case management must step in and manage it.

4.1 Operational Risk

The first step in managing operational risk is to ensure that traders don't enter into deals which cannot be handled by the existing resources and structures of the company. This would include deals in regions where the time difference, language, customs, and lack of contacts pose excessive challenges. Of course, this would not apply to oil majors or the largest trading houses since they have a global presence. Instead this would apply to a smaller regional trader, for example an oil company who has only ever done physical deals on the US West Coast and the US Gulf Coast. It would be foolish for them to enter into a trade with a loading in China and a discharge in East Africa unless there was a compelling reason and a very large potential gain. This does not mean that no company should expand, but the expansion should be accompanied by acquiring expertise in the new markets. This same trading company could, for example, open a small office in Singapore and staff it with an operator and a junior trader with experience in the Asian and African markets.

In addition to the well-known operational risks in physical trading, there are operational risks in trading derivatives.[1] While derivatives are generally standardized (a swap traded in Asia is handled the same way as a swap traded in Europe), this would imply that the company at least has systems in place to manage derivatives. Often, trading companies start out with purely physical deals, usually "risk-free" back-to-back trades. As the company expands, it increases its risk and needs to begin hedging.[2] Ultimately the company will start trading derivatives almost independently of their physical trading. Indeed, most of the large trading companies and the trading departments of the large oil companies have derivative traders and derivative desks who act much the same as their counterparts at hedge funds and investment banks. But accounting for derivative risk is very different from accounting for back-to-back physical risk.

Many companies are content to use spreadsheets to track the risk, but programs like Excel are not designed for this purpose. They are highly susceptible to error since a wrong number in one cell of one sheet could impact the results across the entire file and the entire portfolio. Checking and correcting errors is often difficult since the spreadsheet was probably built by one trader, and only he has full access and understanding of how it works. Back and middle office staff, if they have access to the trades (one would hope so!) might not even understand how the derivatives work; it is foolish to assume they can measure risk and control the activities of the traders if they don't understand the exposure created by a swap or an option. There have been many cases of companies losing millions through a simple lack of understanding of derivatives, though the culprit is more often options than simple swaps and futures contracts.

In 2004 China Aviation Oil, a Singapore-based trading arm of a Chinese aviation company, CAOHC (China Aviation Oil Holding Company based in Beijing), ran up massive losses in options trading. While the head of CAO Singapore was convicted and sent to jail, it was not for the losses but for defrauding his bankers and hiding the losses. CAO had started trading options on a speculative basis. When those trades went wrong, CAO tried to hedge the risk with more options (allegedly on the advice of their principal counterparty, a well-known investment bank, who then traded them the next set of options designed to "help" CAO). CAO ended up losing $550 million.

---

[1] A derivative is a financial instrument or contract which doesn't have any physical delivery. Derivatives are "bets" on prices. This is an analogy, not a definition, since traders don't gamble; they speculate. Derivatives can be used to speculate or to limit risk ("hedge").

[2] Hedging is the act of protecting yourself from losses that result from changes in prices. This will be discussed at length in the chapter on price risk and hedging.

4 Managing Risk

It is clear that few, if any, of the parties at CAO and CAOHC understood the risks, possibly because the systems they had in place did not properly value those risks or present them in a manner that was comprehensible to management.

A more familiar case for most followers of trading scandals and massive losses is the story of Nick Leeson and Barings Bank. Nick Leeson also lost his money by trading options; he lost $1.4 billion (this was in 1995 when that was real money) and bankrupted Barings. While Leeson committed fraud by hiding his losses, the only way he could get away with it was because the bank's managers were clueless about options and had no system in place to monitor his trades. They relied solely on Leeson's emails and phone calls; any reports they received were generated by Leeson. Leeson's activities were certainly criminal, and he paid the price by spending four years in a Singapore prison, but the bank's management was possibly criminally negligent for allowing a trader to run positions they could not evaluate and probably would not understand if they even saw them.

There are several ways to mitigate and manage operational risk, but they all involve having the right people and the right systems in place. This means hiring knowledgeable, reliable traders, operators, and middle office staff. It means having managers and even CEOs who know what swaps and options are and how it creates or hedges risk. It means having a robust, comprehensive system for entering trades, evaluating risk, and presenting it in a coherent, logical manner. Most trading companies, banks, and oil majors spend tens or hundreds of millions either developing or buying back office software systems that track deals, exposure, contracts, and payments. These systems are monitored by professional, empowered middle office employees. Above all, management understands risk and can interpret what they see on the reports generated by the back office systems.

It is difficult to judge if a trader will be successful (make money) before he starts his trading career, but it is typically easier to judge if he is reliable and trustworthy. Unfortunately, the kind of person who is a highly profitable trader is rarely a corporate, team player who obeys the rules. Indeed, trading desks and trading companies promote rule bending and rule breaking. For the most part, though, traders with a modicum of experience don't enter into trades their company can't manage, at least not for physical deals. There is an internal logic to this. A trader wants to make money. If he does a deal that then becomes a disaster because his operators or shipping department don't know how to manage it, he will lose money. However, a new or junior trader will easily and naively enter into difficult to manage trades simply because he does not know any better. Trading companies need to tailor the limits and authority they give to traders as a function of their experience and temperament. An enthusiastic, risk-seeking brand new trader should be required to clear any trade with a senior trader or a manager before concluding the deal. Or the trader could be given a geographical range in which he can trade certain sizes of trades within specific time frames (e.g., the trader is allowed to trade only up to 35,000 MT of standard Euro grade diesel or heating oil for loading/delivery in North West Europe or the Mediterranean and no farther out than sixty days.). The easiest way to fight a fire is to keep it from starting in the first place.

Of course, any deal can go wrong. Most of my readers would probably be at a loss to organize a loading and discharge of a cargo of crude oil from Nigeria to China even if you are oil traders (unless you just got promoted from crude oil operations to a trading desk, of course). There are many documents to be produced as well as a long list of people who must be notified and kept informed all through the loading of the vessel, the voyage to China, and the discharge. It is simple for a trader to buy and sell a cargo; he merely tells a broker "Done!" What happens after that is more complicated. This is why operators at oil companies are not merely typists sending out loading instructions or secretaries relaying information between the finance department and the shipping department. Oil operators are highly skilled and highly paid professionals who often make the difference between successful trading and disasters.

The ideal for many traders is to buy a cargo, resell it, and never hear about it again. When there are professional operators this is possible. Weak or inexperienced operators can make mistakes, forget to send key documents on time, or be hoodwinked by more savvy, cunning counterparts. A good operator will first and foremost minimize losses and protect profits by making sure that each physical cargo is loaded on time and properly (correct quality, quantity, and documents) and that the contracts and financing are all in order. That is purely the reactive part of operations, making certain that things go as smoothly as possible to avoid delays, demurrage, and disputes. Can an operator be a great operator? Yes, by being proactive and even creating opportunities and trades for the trader.

The great operators I have worked with over the years were, of course, professional and reliable in the daily operations of oil trading. They were also commercial and responsible. Great operators can be entrusted with trading decisions that can cost or make millions over the year. As Adi Imsirovic remarked in his recent book Trading and Price Discovery for Crude Oils, some oil operators drive Ferraris, at least those responsible for handling Forward Brent nominations. One operator I worked with negotiated away an annoying and expensive pumping fee imposed by no less than Saudi Aramco. Other operators have provided me information that led to profitable deals including one case where an operator spoke to her counterpart at a refining company and learned the refinery had made a planning error and was desperate to sell a prompt cargo at almost any price; I bought the cargo after "coincidentally and casually" calling the trader at that company. I can't recall the number of times my operators have listened to me negotiating a deal and reminded me of certain difficult conditions with that supplier, buyer, port, or contract (I suppose both my memory and judgment were pretty bad if they had to keep reminding me). I have entrusted operators with making decisions on when to stop loading a cargo based on market conditions. Most of the barge (small vessels of 500 to 5000 metric tonnes) operators I worked with were given authority to charter barges themselves without checking with the traders.

There are many others in a trading company who contribute to managing operational risk including the shipping department, the finance department, and the legal department. How they contribute depends on their competency, experience, and intelligence. The key to managing operational risk is to spend as much time, money, and energy hiring excellent back office staff as you do hiring traders.

4.2 Contractual Risk

Contracts are not written out and argued over at length by lawyers, barristers, and judges simply because we don't trust each other. For the most part, trading is about trust, at least as far as a trader's word goes. When a trader commits to a deal, it is usually only after discussing a few key elements of the contract, but we nonetheless assume the trader will honor the deal from that moment forward, including during the time when the formal, written contract has not yet been exchanged. This is not simply a question of good faith, saving face, or respect; a trader's word is his bond in both a moral and legal sense as we discussed earlier. For the most part, traders enter into agreements with the intent of honoring them and complying with the terms and conditions. When a trader fails to respect the contract, he might accept responsibility if it is his fault (and the cost is not too large). So why do we need a written contract?

Written contracts exist because often things go wrong that are nobody's fault. Contracts are not about assigning blame but about defining responsibilities. If a cargo is struck by a meteorite, it is unlikely to be anyone's fault, least of all the trader sitting in his office in Geneva or Singapore. But the Gods and Fates who aim and fling chunks of rock around the universe don't care if it's the trader's fault; neither does the contract. The contract instead says that it is his responsibility. So an unlucky trader whose cargo is destroyed by a rock from space might lose millions when he has to replace the cargo to fulfill his DAP contract (DAP is an Incoterm which means "delivered at place." Many of you might be familiar with the old expression "Delivered Ex-Ship."). It seems unlikely that any trader would be happy about such a situation and would certainly try to argue that it was not his fault so he should not have to pay. The contract would likely say otherwise. So a contract is written to make sure everyone complies with the terms and conditions and pays for breaches of those terms and conditions even when it is not their fault.

The notions of fault and responsibility are concepts which are key to choosing a governing law for a contract. The preferred law and, by logical extension, jurisdiction are English law and the English legal system (courts or arbitration) not only because of the long history of international commercial law (what is called jurisprudence) but because an overriding principle of English commercial law is to find settlements which respect the fundamental intent of the disputed contract and allow commerce to continue. So in the case of the meteorite, the English court might force the trader to make good on his commitment and deliver a cargo to the buyer in addition to paying the buyer's legal fees.

An American court might do the same but also assess punitive damages against the trader for being unlucky or displeasing the Gods and therefore harming his client (okay, that is perhaps far fetched but the bias is clear; US courts are more open to punitive damages and litigious behavior.). In the case of an English court, the trader might lose ten million on the cost of the cargo and two million in legal fees. In the American court, the trader could lose ten million in trading costs, two million in legal fees and a further fifty million in punitive damages.

In reality, there is not really "US law." Each state has its own set of common law though all adhere to and apply the Uniform Commercial Code. When parties choose a US jurisdiction for international contracts, they typically choose New York law and a court in New York. Other legal systems like Singapore are being used increasingly.

English law remains the law of choice and the jurisdiction of choice for additional reasons:

- it is well understood and widely and historically used (British Empire's lasting mark);

- it has a principle of legal certainty: you get what the contract says you should get;
- high quality of the jurisdictions: experienced and knowledgeable judges and arbitrators; and
- recovery of costs wherein the loser pays the winner's costs.[3]

So the first step in managing contractual risk is to enter into clear, full contracts written in an appropriate language and referring to almost all conceivable eventualities, including things like meteorites. Pending developments with the Lugano Accords and Britain's relationship with the European Union, the best language for contracts is English, the best law is English law, and the best jurisdiction is the English legal system. From that base, the contract needs to then cover everything that might worry the trader, the finance department, the shipping department, the middle office, the marketing department, the legal department and management. Of course, it also needs to be acceptable to counterparties so it cannot be unduly biased, unbalanced, or unfair or it will be rejected. A contract that contains a clause which reads "The Seller takes no responsibility for anything and will never have to pay for any losses, costs or consequences of any kind no matter what he does or does not do" might make the seller's legal department ecstatic but it would be instantly rejected by the buyer. Instead the two parties agree to a contract which covers the rights, obligations, and responsibilities as defined by the principles of commerce (what is a buyer, what is a seller) and the rules and guidelines outlined by things like Incoterms, jurisprudence, experience, and common sense.

The traders rarely, if ever, go over each term, clause, and condition of the contract when they negotiate a deal. Instead they agree the key elements and then further agree to use a contract both companies accept. This could be a long-form contract (complete contract with all the various clauses, terms, and conditions included) that was previously agreed or it could be general terms and conditions published by one of their companies or another company. So a trader from Vitol who buys a cargo from Glencore could conclude a deal which uses BP's General Terms and Conditions for the Sale and Purchase of Crude Oil and Oil Products.[4] If no GT&Cs are mentioned, then the unspecified clauses are typically covered by Incoterms (which are much more than

---

[3] With great thanks to Joseph Magoon of Squire, Patton, Boggs for his help in explaining English, US, and NY law to me.

[4] Large oil private and national oil companies tend to have their own General Terms and Conditions (GT&Cs) which they use for their contracts. GT&Cs are published and dated. If BP publishes their GT&Cs, they cannot suddenly amend them to include onerous clauses without consulting with counterparties and getting their approval of the new contract.

mere three letter abbreviations like FOB and CIF). Contracts and GT&Cs evolve to reflect both changing market conditions and the market's experience with disputes. Take, for example, the Force Majeure clause which is included in nearly all oil contracts.

Force Majeure is something that many people understand intuitively but can't necessarily define precisely. It's "something bad that's not my fault and out of my control which makes me unable to perform the contract." It is important to note that Force Majeure is not something which makes the contract onerous, costly or loss-making, at least within certain limits. If you sell someone a cargo and then discover you are losing ten dollars per tonne on the deal, that is not a valid reason for declaring Force Majeure.[5] On the other hand, if you could replace a lost cargo but it would cost several million dollars or more, then it might be a valid reason (assuming the original cargo was lost because of a Force Majeure situation).

Sometimes Force Majeure is defined as an Act of God: an unpredictable, unavoidable, and overwhelming event which causes a major breach despite the best will and efforts of the trader. These ideas are simple to understand but harder to define with precision. For this reason, typical Force Majeure clauses provide a definition as well as a very long, non-exhaustive list of what might constitute Force Majeure. Most are obvious, such as war, insurrection, earthquakes, fires, floods, strikes, and embargoes. Some are oddly specific [in the case of BP's Force Majeure clause which includes compliance with any law of any authority "including the International Energy Agency (IEA)"]. The length of the Force Majeure clause and the inclusion of so many examples grew out of jurisprudence and experience. It is likely that BP experienced losses when a counterparty declared Force Majeure because of a decision of the IEA. BP's standard contract now includes that example not just to make certain they are covered by IEA-based Force Majeure but to make certain they are protected by orders, demands, and requests of any agency similar to the IEA. BP's clause is five sections long with many sub-sections and takes up an entire page of their GT&Cs. Obviously, for BP, simply saying that Force Majeure is an "act of God" which stops one of the parties from performing is not adequate for their risk management.

Drawing up an acceptable and complete (as possible) contract is the first step in managing contractual risk. Managing that risk still depends on having a legal department that understands what is written, a trader who understands how the contract applies to his deal and an operator who understands the

---

[5] Traders refer to this as "Price Majeure." When a trader is losing too much money on a deal, he will logically try to find any way out of it. The Force Majeure clause is broad and somewhat fuzzy so it is often invoked for what is really "price majeure."

contract in order to carry it out and comply with it. Unfortunately, this is not enough to end trading disputes.

When a deal falls apart (there is a breach of contract) and the dispute cannot be resolved amicably by the traders, it will end up in litigation (in court or in arbitration). At that point the success or failure of the case will depend on the people arguing for and against. Oil companies typically employ outside legal experts to analyze, prepare, and argue their case in court. These lawyers and barristers are experts in commercial law and often well-versed in oil trading. They understand the rules and regulations for presenting a case. They know where to find expert help for technical issues such as market value, shipping operations, and oil quality. Of course, this expert legal representation is not cheap. Legal and court fees for trading disputes can run into millions of dollars. The alternatives, hiring a cheap lawyer or representing yourself (if that is even allowed), are usually a recipe for disaster. Even with the best legal representation from a top international law firm, the most incisive and ruthless pleading from a top London barrister, and technical evidence from an array of oil and trading experts, the final decision is in the hands of the judge or the arbitrators. Even what appears to a trader to be simple, obvious conclusions are not so clear or obvious to a judge who interprets the contract and jurisprudence in an unexpected manner.

A recent case I worked on as an expert was ruled against the defendant; the decision was overturned quickly and decisively on appeal, something which the lawyers assured me would happen because the judge had made a ruling that went against jurisprudence and contract law. What if the appeals court judge had been of the same opinion as the original judge? It is probable that any judge in any jurisdiction will have very limited experience in oil trading whatever their experience in international commerce; if you pin your chance of winning on the expectation that a septuagenarian judge on his first oil case will understand the finer points of kurtosis in option pricing, you might be disappointed.

A final point about disputes and jurisdiction. As I said, an English High Court (the Commercial Court) case is presided over by a judge who may or may not understand oil markets. Lawyers and traders have been surprised by decisions over recent years. Additionally, Commercial Court proceedings are costly and formal. Instead, and this is the advice of top lawyers in London, it would be better to choose arbitration in London. An arbitration panel is typically composed of three arbitrators. Each side in the dispute chooses one arbitrator who in turn choose a third to preside. It would be strange if each side did not choose an arbitrator with experience in oil markets and trading. Those two would likely choose a third arbitrator with similar experience. Of course, it could be said that there might be an advantage to arguing a case in front of a judge or arbitrator who doesn't understand trading, but that is more about perverting justice than mitigating losses and respecting markets and commerce!

As I finish writing this, a fresh opinion from one law firm is that the High Court might be better after all. They have been disappointed by arbitration decisions (sour grapes on the part of the lawyers?) and have noticed that arbitration costs have risen sharply, making arbitration even more costly than court. It confirms my advice that traders are better off avoiding lawsuits entirely and settling disputes over a beer or a cup of coffee![6]

4.3 Legal Risk

Companies regularly weigh legal consequences against profits, and this is indeed the first step in managing legal risks. The business model of American banks has been to write the laws and rules in the first place, undermine oversight and reform, confuse and obstruct regulators, legislators, and clients, and finally simply accept the occasional fine as a cost of doing business. It is rare to see a banker go to jail. If this were not true, then we would not recognize names like Nick Leeson or Bernie Madoff; they would be just another convict in a long line of criminals sent to jail for various banking crimes. And even if a few bankers are sent to jail (exactly one banker was jailed for crimes committed during the Financial Crisis of 2007–2009), the banks are left untouched aside from token fines. With politicians in their pockets and literally hundreds of billions of dollars at their disposal, banks agree to pay fines without admitting guilt. In most other areas of life, this would be considered a bribe; in finance, it is the cost of doing business. "Business" includes bribery, money laundering, fraud, theft, misrepresentation, market manipulation, and excessive risk-taking (knowing that the government will bail them out if it goes wrong). It would be foolish to the extreme for a bank to not act criminally or at least immorally. Does the same apply to oil trading?

The answer is a resounding "yes". Oil markets are historically and inherently corrupt. While most traders do not commit what could be considered criminal acts, most at least lie daily since that is an essential part of negotiating. Lying during a negotiation leads to lying when discussing the market

---

[6] When you consider that a good lawyer (or solicitor as they are called in England) charges £600 to £900 per hour and most cases involve a few lawyers, some juniors and some clerks, it is clear that legal fees can be astronomical. On top of that there are fees for court or arbitration as well as outside experts. Then there is the value of the time lost by the traders, operators, legal department, and management of the companies involved in the dispute.

("spinning the market") in an attempt to move prices one way or another. All of this is legal for the most part or at least it is extremely hard to prove criminal intent or fraud. In the US, telling a reporter or another trader that you are bullish is an opinion protected by the First Amendment. Reporting only bullish information and keeping silent on bearish data is perfectly legal. Many other countries have similar protections for simple opinions. Trading companies accept this as part of the normal activity of oil trading. Profits justify "immoral and corrupt" day-to-day practices in trading that would not be accepted in most other areas of our society.

From casual lying about your positions to bribing and cheating is a slippery slope which, as I said, most traders don't slide down. That said, senior management and many traders who do not commit criminal acts are nonetheless aware of them taking place in their company. If traders and trading companies are rarely convicted of bribery and corruption, those who fail to report the activity are, as far as I know, wholly untouched and never brought up in proceedings even when criminal charges are made. Consequently, for a trading company, it is easy and usual to blame a lone bad apple for illegal activities in the market while maintaining the corporate line that the company is shocked by the allegations, claims that they are unacceptable to the company, and is committed to abiding by all rules and guidelines, etc. In the event a trader is caught and convicted, the company will possibly end up paying fines but will rarely need to worry about senior management getting charged. One wonders how some trading companies function at all when a "rogue trader" is allowed to pay out tens of millions in bribes from the corporate accounts without management knowing!

The temptation to cheat is immense in oil trading. Trading is all about making money, and making money in oil trading is not always easy. Paradoxically, as traders made record amounts in recent years, they also say the market has become extremely hard to trade. Indeed, the market has become much more transparent and liquid over the years with increased competition among the largest traders and from the trading arms of national oil companies. Competition has driven down margins in the largest, most liquid markets or pushed smaller companies out altogether.

An easy way to make money in oil trading, or any business, is to cheat and steal. In fact, the easiest way to make money is just to be lucky, but that can't be guaranteed in the long run. No one can make a living by playing roulette every day for forty years unless they have rigged the wheel or owned the casino. The top oil companies and trading companies did not build up their fortunes by being honest; they bribed and cheated their way to control the markets in oil exploration, refining, downstream, and trading. They built empires using their home country's military and foreign services. Why work hard to understand markets, build up an expert team of traders, and struggle to make a few dollars trading cargoes of crude oil you bought at market prices when you can slip an oil minister a few million dollars and get a contract well under the market price? You can make hundreds of millions in profits without breaking a sweat.[7]

Trading companies have been prominently in the news recently because of major scandals in Brazil, Mexico, Singapore, and Nigeria. According to ViolationTracker, an anti-corruption web site, Vitol has paid $166 million in fines and penalties related to corruption since 2000. Glencore has paid over $1.5 billion in fines and restitution related to bribery and corruption in 2022 alone. Both trading companies have posted profits from hundreds of millions to billions a year from trading over the past two decades. While Vitol's recent massive fine for its involvement in corruption in Brazil, Mexico, and Ecuador might make headlines, it hardly makes a dent in the bottom line. It would surprise me if Vitol's CEO saw any reduction in pay linked to this fine. So fines are nothing more than an annoyance for trading companies, at least until the fines are increased so as to make corruption unprofitable. Or until governments stop accepting plea bargains involving no admission of guilt and instead hold, as they should, the entire company liable and fine and even imprison senior management. Until that happens, oil trading companies will manage legal risk by staying within certain boundaries.

Murder and destruction are no longer generally contemplated, for example, though they were once part and parcel of the oil business. Traditional criminality such as bribery and falsifying documents is acceptable as long as it is not too overt and ideally outside the legal authority of the US. Mexico has recently announced a ban on Vitol and Glencore from all oil business in that country. This might be a deterrent, but based on my experience in the market, both of those companies will find a way to continue doing business there either through shell corporations or silent partnerships with acceptable companies. It is even likely that Vitol will soon return to Mexico since they have recently provided a list of all the Pemex employees they bribed over the years. It remains to be seen if this is Vitol turning over a new life or cynically tossing their former corrupted clients to the wolves to be allowed to stay in the game.

This point of view might seem cynical and even shocking to many readers, including many who are in the oil business, but it is certainly the reality of the business. For those of you with morals and a healthy fear of fines and prison

---

[7] I am not accusing all oil companies of being corrupt or having been founded corruptly, but the history of oil industry and recent reporting about major trading companies demonstrate my point.

terms, there are further steps you can take to manage legal risk. All you have to do is follow the sound advice trading companies give after one of their employees has been caught: claim it was an exception, make an announcement that the company abhors this behavior and that the company is taking steps to improve its oversight and behavior, and solemnly swear this certainly won't happen again…until next time. So how do you put these hollow words into effect and truly manage legal risk?

Most banks and trading companies have structures in place to monitor and control the activity of traders. This is called the Middle Office and can be considered in many ways the Internal Affairs Department of trading or the internal police. One of the functions of the Middle Office is to make certain traders comply with internal and external rules and regulations as well as respect the limits set on their trading (how much risk they can take on). This function is called Compliance.

The Compliance department monitors positions, trades, and prices to make sure that the trader and the company overall are not exceeding the stated limits (internal and external). For example, if a trader has a risk limit of $5 million of Value-At-Risk,[8] compliance will calculate the trader's VAR every day to make sure it is within that limit. The Compliance department will also monitor position sizes relative to third parties including exchanges. Exchanges usually have position limits to avoid letting one company dominate, squeeze, or manipulate the market. Compliance should be monitoring positions to make sure they don't exceed the official exchange limits before those limits are reached.

Compliance will also be involved in checking counterparties as part of Know Your Client (KYC) and Anti-Money Laundering (AML) in cooperation with the finance department. Compliance might also monitor positions with counterparties to make certain that they are all above board and have valid market justifications. Compliance is also responsible for making certain that traders are reporting correct and accurate market prices for their positions. A trader might be tempted to hide losses by entering false prices into the system or to boost his bonus in the same manner. Compliance should find independent sources for market prices to cross-check the trader's inputs. This is not always simple.

---

[8] VAR is "Value At Risk" which is a statistical measure of how much a trader could hypothetically lose overnight or over a day on his positions. It is a measure of potential loss based on statistical probability and degrees of confidence in price movements. A VAR of 95% with 15% asset risk means that on one out of twenty days the positions could lose 15% of their value. VAR measures historical movements and cannot predict Black Swans.

Market prices for prompt and liquid underlyings like physical cargoes and futures contracts are easy to check. Compliance need only read Platts[9] or log onto ICE to check the market prices. Other prices are not so easy. Where would you find prices for Calendar 2026 Mean of Platts Japan (MOPJ) Naphtha swaps? How about June 2027 $35 Puts on Dubai crude oil? For the MOPJ Naphtha swaps it would be relatively easy to ask brokers in Singapore or Tokyo for copies of their reports. For the Dubai options, it is nearly impossible to find a source for their value; the only place to find volatility reports (Implied Volatility, a value used for pricing and trading options) for June '27 would be on Brent or WTI options and then probably only for At-the-Money options.[10] Valuing deep out-of-the-money options is as much art as science so there is much more leeway for a trader to misrepresent his positions. In all of the cases, the Compliance officer needs to understand what the trader is doing in the first place in order to calculate his risk (VAR or whatever measurement a company might use).

When I worked for an investment bank I was called by the CEO of the bank who wanted to know why I was trying to destroy his bank like some Nick Leeson wannabe. He had received a disturbing report from the Middle Office that I was exceeding my VAR limit by several orders of magnitude (hundred of millions of dollars of VAR). His call was not wholly unexpected since I had been called by everyone below him in the chain and had explained myself at length; no one understood what was going on so they passed the problem up the chain. I explained once again to the CEO that I was not a rogue trader and that the VAR calculation was wrong. My position was, in fact, exceedingly small and not even a small percentage of my trading limit. The problem lay with the Middle Office; they had entered bad historical prices for the three months up to that date and so created the impression that the market in consideration (Singapore high sulfur fuel oil swaps) was wildly volatile, exceeding even Bitcoin or Pets.com in price swings. The calculations based on the erroneous prices meant that according to the back office computer, the price of fuel oil in Singapore could rise or fall by several thousand dollars overnight, leading to hundreds of millions in potential losses. I explained to the CEO that the math was correct but the numbers were wrong ("Garbage In, Garbage Out," as programmers say). The back office system

---

[9] Platts is the short-hand name for S&P Global Platts market reports. Platts is a Price Reporting Agency (PRA), a private company which publishes market prices for oil and other commodities. The most common way to assess the price of oil and invoice it is by using the prices published by Platts. Other PRA's exist such as Argus and Opis.

[10] This is not a book on option trading, and I apologize for tossing in this vocabulary without warning. The internet is filled with resources which explain options. Alternatively, I can recommend Neil Schofield's book Commodity Derivatives (Wiley Finance, 2007).

had corrupt prices (which should have been Platts prices ranging from $300 to $325 per metric tonne over the period but instead moved randomly up and down from as low as Minus $30,000 to as high as $50,000 per metric tonne). The CEO accepted my explanation and did not fire me after all. What does this tell us about compliance?

Garbage In, Garbage Out! If the Compliance department is stocked with incompetent people who don't understand trading, they won't be able to carry out their jobs. Indeed, many companies in oil trading and banking intentionally hire "incompetent" compliance officers or at least structure their job and power to insure a minimum of intervention. When I worked for a trading company in London they hired a compliance officer who was hardly an idiot and who had extensive experience in international financial fraud and crime; he had risen through the ranks in the New York Police Department where he was in charge of art crime and financial fraud, later joining various FBI financial fraud task forces and ultimately working with Interpol on financial fraud and money laundering. Of course, he had no experience in oil trading and no understanding of markets or pricing. He looked great on paper and demonstrated that the company was committed to compliance, having brought in a real cop with over thirty years of experience in financial crimes. As far as I can recall during my years at the company, not a single trader was ever "fingered by compliance" for any crimes or rule breaking. A compliance department is only as good as its employees and the skills and powers they are given to verify and enforce the limits and rules.

If a trading company were serious about compliance, it would hire a real trader with some decades of experience in just the sort of things they are trying to stop and also pay him a very large salary with bonuses for everything he stops or prevents. The Compliance department would need to be adequately staffed and given authority to examine all accounts and materials for which they are nominally responsible. This is not typically the case; a senior manager's desk, safe, or computer might be off limits to compliance. If a company is serious about operating legally, no one's office or systems should be safe from oversight by compliance.

Another tool for managing legal risk is to hire honest traders. It is hard to say who is going to be corrupted by the market when a company hires a crop of new graduates, but it is certainly known or suspected by the market at large when a trader or a company is already corrupt. Often the temptation is too great, though, and the upside to hiring a trader with experience at a trading company with a reputation for dodgy dealing is greater than the risks of what he might do once hired. I have often heard managers defending employing erratic, high-risk, or dodgy traders by saying the trader is a great trader who makes lots of money and the manager is smart and tough enough to control the trader, unlike the managers in the trader's previous companies. It usually ends up badly. A company that truly believes in its stated values should have a quasi-zero tolerance policy for immorality and corruption.

Zero tolerance is hard in oil trading. How can you tell your traders not to lie when it is an essential negotiating tool? The simplest step is to limit what they can say to certain people like reporters, consultants, and outside authorities. As a consultant and occasional expert witness for trading disputes, I rely on traders for up-to-date information on the market or advice on certain aspects of the market for a legal case I might be working on. When I was trading it was easy to call up another trader and chat about the market even when calling someone I had never spoken to before. These days, following various pricing scandals and investigations into market manipulation, traders are under fairly strict instructions to talk to no one about anything other than what is necessary for their trading. If the traders cannot comment on the market to outside sources, and this includes Platts, Reuters, Argus, etc., they cannot lie, spin, or manipulate the market; this protects the company from allegations of market manipulation. This does not prevent a trader from "lying" to another trader by claiming the market is very bullish and that prices will most certainly rise soon; this is considered opinion and is generally treated as protected speech. Indeed it would be a sad day when a trader had to start negotiations by telling his potential buyer that he believed the market was weak and that he needed to sell his cargo as quickly and cheaply as possible before things get worse.

Zero tolerance can be extended to all areas of trading including simple book-keeping. Years ago I was told that at J. Aron (commodity division of Goldman Sachs) traders are fined if they enter their trades incorrectly into the back office system. The first error is fined a token amount like $50,000 (taken out of the trader's profits). The second error is double that fine plus a dressing down by the local Compliance officer. The third error is a fine of $250,000 plus a trip to corporate headquarters in New York to explain why the trader is an idiot (the round-trip ticket allows only for time to go to the office, get yelled at, and then return to the airport, assuming the trader works outside of New York).[11] It is clear that J. Aron takes compliance seriously, at least as far as protecting senior management's bonuses goes. I am not convinced that Goldman's approach to compliance is the same when it comes to external dealings with clients and the market, but I leave the reader to do his own research on Goldman's activities and reputation.

---

[11] The amounts shown are not necessarily the real fines imposed by J Aron but are indicative of the overall approach and philosophy.

A trading company that is serious about compliance could start with a J. Aron type model and extend that to cover all aspects of trading including external relationships and behavior on the market. Random drug and alcohol tests might result in dozens, if not hundreds, of traders being fired, though in all fairness the culture of long, booze-filled lunches has changed over the years. Up until the mid-2000s it was common for oil traders to come back and trade after a two or three hour lunch when they were certainly over the legal limit for driving. One company I worked for instituted a policy that said traders who drank at lunch should not report back to work (I think Exxon had been the first to start this). It is not always obvious when a trader is inebriated, though, so enforcing that policy is difficult. While some banks might have random drug testing, I am not aware of any trading company or trading arm of any oil company that tests its employees at any time. I believe the investment banks do it, at least in the US. A coke-head trader who drinks at lunch is a recipe for disaster no matter how great that trader has been. Perhaps Breathalyzer tests should be added to the panoply of checkpoints and passwords that restrict access to trading floors, phones, and trading applications these days.

Assuming that everyone in the company is sober and honest, there are probably few things to worry about. That said, it is not always clear to traders or managers that certain activities are illegal. Bribes might be illegal but "facilitating payments" are sometimes acceptable if that is the way business is done. US law, for example, allows for small payments designed to smooth and expedite routine administrative processes that would otherwise take place anyway but at a slower pace. Slipping a few dollars to a clerk in the immigration office to speed up the processing of a work permit that is already approved is not a bribe in legal terms. But the line between facilitating payment and bribe is blurry and moves from country to country or company to company. It also leads to a slippery slope where paying officials to make sure documents are produced quickly so a vessel can sail without delay turns into larger sums to change the date on a bill of lading because "it's only a few minutes difference." How can we tell when a payment is a facilitating payment and legal or a bribe and illegal?

I once knew a young entrepreneur who paid some money to secure a contract to clean and wax the floors of a thirty story office building. The handover took place in a dim basement parking lot. The money was carried in a brown paper grocery bag and few words were spoken. This Cold War spy scenario was a pretty good indicator that the transaction was illegal. The sum involved was also not a minor facilitating payment; it was $30,000 (this was back in 1982 when this was a decent amount of money). It would take an unrealistically naive trader to think this was above board and legal.

When I teach about risk and discuss personal and legal risk, I try to explain the difference between cooperation (generally a legal activity) and collusion (commonly considered illegal). The complexities of the legal definition according to various jurisdictions are best left to lop lawyers and judges. I tell my students that if they are talking to another company about a deal or arrangement in the office using the (recorded) land line, it is probably cooperation. If, on the other hand, they are discussing the deal on a personal cell phone or in a dimly lit alley behind a bar, it is probably collusion. This distinction depends on the trader being able to differentiate between the two as well; if the company tacitly encourages corruption or if senior management actively and openly carries it out, then younger, inexperienced traders might believe that what they are doing is not wrong or at least is acceptable and common practice.

This defense of collusion and corruption was put forth by traders in the LIBOR scandal. The defendants claimed it was how the market worked and everyone did it. I doubt they thought it was okay to manipulate LIBOR but some probably honestly believed that while it was not "strictly legal," it was not really a crime. Certainly the trail of evidence suggests that the manipulation was discussed in a more or less open manner and not in back alleys. It would be generous to a fault and naive to believe that management at these banks was not aware of how traders ran the LIBOR market. It is more likely that management taught these traders how to operate in the first place and were complicit in the manipulation as they raked in their share of the bonuses.

Corruption and cheating are seemingly irrepressible and endemic. Given the nature of the business, trading companies need to pick and choose their traders and their markets with care. In addition to an empowered and experienced compliance department, it might be prudent to avoid certain markets with reputations for questionable practices. This might include certain African or South American countries like Nigeria or Brazil.[12] Certainly there has been massive corruption in both of those markets, but the overall amount of money made or paid likely pales in comparison to the amounts made illegally in liquid, transparent markets in Europe, Singapore, and the US over the years. The difference between those kinds of markets is that it is possible to trade profitably in Singapore or New York Harbor without being corrupt.

---

[12] Brazil is claiming to have cleaned up its national oil company and oil politics. Nigeria has been either trying or claiming to try to clean up its oil markets for decades; the Nigerian market appears to be in a "clean" phase which is a relative term, of course.

Oversight of those markets has increased as financial regulators, national and local governments, and market participants themselves raise red flags and bring charges of manipulation and corruption. It is nonetheless likely that at least a small part of the "first world" markets like Singapore and Rotterdam are manipulated every day. Recently a former Glencore trader admitted to manipulating the Los Angeles fuel oil market from 2012 to 2016. It is not at all surprising to me that this trader manipulated the market. Instead, it surprises me that he was caught. And while this trader apparently directed others to make bids and offers in the market to move prices up and down, which is collusion and conspiracy, many traders do the same thing independently (i.e., without colluding with other companies) with the same goal. It has always been illegal to collude but moving the market independently was usually considered as bold, aggressive trading and "part of the game."

Tom Bower, in his excellent book The Squeeze, recounts how John Deuss (Transworld Oil) bought up most of the cargoes on the Brent market back in the late '80s (this is called a "short squeeze"; the buyer then holds the market to ransom, forces prices up and sells at a profit). While the market did not appreciate Deuss's squeeze, it was not considered illegal. Deuss ended up losing $600 million when he tried it again, so perhaps the market thought that a small fine on top of his massive trading losses would be pointless and cruel. The last big short squeeze on the Brent market was already two decades ago in 2002 when Sempra bought almost an entire month's production.[13] In 2007 BP was accused of manipulating part of the US propane market, and while BP ended up paying a hefty fine ($303 million, the largest in CFTC[14] history at the time (This record was beaten in 2020 by, unsurprisingly, a bank), no criminal charges were brought against the traders themselves since they carried out their trading in an over-the-counter, unregulated market. The encouraging news is that these kinds of manipulations and corruption are no longer acceptable and are being prosecuted from various directions.

I have already discussed regulatory and criminal oversight (fines and criminal charges) which appear to be increasing in frequency and leading to more admissions of guilt and convictions as regulatory and criminal authorities increase their understanding of how trading works. Other market participants are also acting to keep markets less dishonest. Platts has worked hard, led by the much maligned Jorge Montepeque at the time, to change the way prices are set in order to prevent manipulation. Indeed, if the Sempra Brent squeeze

---

[13] See Imsirovic, Trading and Price Discovery for Crude Oils.
[14] CFTC: Commodities and Futures Trading Commission, the regulatory authority for commodity trading in the US, at least for regulated futures markets and physical markets.

of 2002 was the last of its kind it is mainly because Platts (under Montepeque's leadership) subsequently added more crude oil to the Brent market, making it much harder for one trader to corner the market. Platts has also changed the way it assesses prices for crude and products; all the prices are now set during a half-hour trading period called the Platts Window. This system is designed to standardize the market, prevent phony trades, and make price discovery transparent and honest. It has improved things significantly.

It is clear that only increased external pressure including holding management responsible and imposing truly dissuasive fines and penalties on companies will clean up the markets. Perhaps a "Three Strikes and Your Out" system could work; any company found guilty of market crimes would be banned from any market that is a signatory to such measures. If Mexico were a signatory of such an agreement, some trading companies could find themselves banned from every country which is also a signatory. Or governments could impose RICO-like statutes. Under RICO (Racketeering and Corrupt Influence Organization), US authorities can dismantle a criminal organization and seize all its assets. Applied worldwide, this would mean that a trading company which commits illegal acts in any one country could have its assets seized in another as well as having senior management held criminally and civilly liable. This is unlikely to happen judging by how governments have handled the banking sector over the years. Perhaps oil majors and large trading companies are "too big to fail". Meanwhile, senior management would need to take a proactive role and aim for a Near-Zero Tolerance Policy for illegal and immoral behavior. Since most senior management I know in the business got there the old-fashioned way, this change will be slow in coming!

4.4 Payment Risk

Oil deals typically involve millions of dollars so not getting paid on even a small number of deals is not acceptable. The industry has already created or applied many methods to ensure that invoices are paid. These include letters of credit, pre-payments, parent company guarantees, collateral, and limits on unprotected risk. In order for these tools to work, the trading company must have a robust and professional finance and accounting department as well as a back office system that is designed for oil trading. In my own career, I have avoided payments on several deals for anywhere from a few days to a few years because the seller simply never sent an invoice. They either had no dedicated back office system or the system was defective. These days it is rare that a company simply forgets to invoice, but it is still possible for invoices to be sent late or incorrectly, leading to delays in payment and lost interest.

Market participants usually point to letters of credit being the ultimate tool to limit payment risk. While it is true that an accurate, well-written, and valid letter of credit issued (or confirmed) by a first class international bank is a fairly certain guaranty of payment, its usefulness depends on knowing all the details of the underlying transactions and the financial condition of the counterparty. Recent scandals in the Singapore trading market have demonstrated that having a letter of credit is not necessarily a guaranty if the letter of credit has been issued fraudulently. In the case of Hin Leong, a large private trading, shipping, and bunkering company based in Singapore, letters of credit from different banks were issued for the same oil or for non-existent cargoes. In simple terms, it appears that Hin Leong sold the same cargoes to several buyers and received letters of credit and payment from multiple banks. This is, if proved, bank fraud. It remains to be seen if Hin Leong's partners will have to foot the bill or if the banks will be forced to make good on all the payments. The case is not as simple as it might appear since it addresses the very foundation and "sanctity" of letters of credit and letters of indemnity.

Following the Hin Leong bankruptcy and other similar cases involving Hontop and Zenrock (also Singapore-based traders), banks and traders have begun to ask how to improve the security of letters of credit. One proposal involves using a central database which banks (and possibly traders) would access to see if the oil in the deal has already been sold or pledged against a loan. Additionally, traders and banks are trying to move to digital documents (using block chain technology). Digital, secure documents would eliminate problems with producing cargo documents. Cargo documents (such as bills of lading, certificates of quality, certificates of quality, certificates of origin, etc.) are required to draw on the letter of credit. Historically the original documents never reach the bank in time for payment to be made. Instead, payment is made against copies of the documents along with a promise to try to find the originals. Mercuria and ING carried out the first all-digital block chain oil cargo deal back in 2017. Today, there are many more deals being carried out on such platforms as Komgo using Trakk, a block chain program developed by Mitsubishi. Block chain documentation should, in theory, prevent the use of fraudulent and falsified documents; the contracts and shipping documents are all transmitted and stored in a secure, digital fashion. This way, no letter of indemnity is required and all the submitted documents proving that the oil was delivered are original and faithful.[15]

---

[15] The use of block chain would also benefit shipowners. Shipowners are asked to discharge cargoes without the formal, original documents. Instead, they discharge against letters of indemnity. When

Of course, this requires that the beneficiary of the letter of credit cannot issue fraudulent documents in the first place. In the case of Hin Leong, the company was both the beneficiary of the letter of credit and the carrier (shipowner) of the cargo. It was therefore easy for Hin Leong to (allegedly) issue fraudulent documents. For this reason, a group of banks involved in financing oil trading led by Standard Bank and DBS Bank, have formed the Trade Finance Registry. The TFR is a blockchain database that allows the participating banks to check if any document has already been submitted for financing purposes. A next step would involve including the trading companies themselves in the registry though this poses challenges for privacy and market information. This would also probably not address problems arising from sales made without letters of credit (i.e., the company has sold the cargo once on open credit and again using a letter of credit), but it is big step in reducing financing fraud.

There is a requirement in trading to Know Your Client (KYC). KYC goes hand in hand with anti-money laundering (AML). Some large trading companies are privately held, though, and do not publish results or make their financing public. Even if a trader is certain that the beneficial owners of his counterparty are not Al Qaeda or the Russian Mob, he will still have a hard time verifying the financial solidity and legal status of the company. This task is already difficult for large, publicly listed corporations; Enron is a perfect example since it was the darling of Wall Street and the energy markets all while being a deeply, fundamentally corrupt Ponzi scheme. Other companies may be solid today and collapse tomorrow.

When I was working for a company in Singapore, I asked my finance department for a certain amount of open credit for Hin Leong (i.e., they could buy oil from us without opening letters of credit up to a certain dollar limit). The head of finance visited the offices of Hin Leong and spent the day going over their private accounts; after looking over their accounts and bank statements, he gave them a sizeable trading limit. Since that time Hin Leong's business has expanded significantly and I would guess that the limit was increased (or at least not reduced) without the company rechecking the books. The increases would likely have been based on Hin Leong's volumes of trades, apparent assets (ships, storage terminals, barges, and oil in tank), and reputation. There has been little public disclosure of losses made by companies who extended unsecured trading credit to Hin Leong, but it would

---

there is fraud and the cargo has been pledged or sold to multiple parties, the shipowner can be held liable for the value of the oil. Block chain hypothetically allows the market to confirm the existence of one true cargo and one true owner. That said, advances in quantum computing now mean that the block chain is no longer quasi-invulnerable to hacking.

be naive to assume that only the banks issuing the letters of credit were defrauded in Hin Leong's collapse. So, KYC requires an ongoing, thorough check of counterparties, something that is onerous in time, money, and relationships. But as the Soviets and Americans decreed for the SALT treaties, "Trust, but verify." Oil trading, unfortunately, cannot be verified with a few passes of high-altitude spy planes or satellites. Traders will always be at risk of payment defaults caused by fraud or honest failure.

4.5 Personal Risk

My advice to the students in my commodity trading classes is to be careful when going into trading. This falls on deaf ears, of course, since trading is glamorous, prestigious, and well-paid. There is a strong attraction to the lifestyle as well as the job. People who are attracted to the glamor of the job more than the job itself are at high risk of falling into the pitfalls I discussed earlier. If you tie your self-worth up in the result of your last trade, you become very vulnerable. So, if you decide to become a trader, how do you manage the personal risks?

The first step is to carefully choose who you work for and with. If you love buying and selling oil but don't want to end up with liver failure and a third wife by the age of forty, you might want to choose to work for Exxon or Shell. A second step would be to remain in your own country where you are more emotionally comfortable and stable to begin with. You have easy access to family and friends who are unlikely to be in the oil business and therefore less likely to facilitate bad behavior. Young traders who get sent to exotic locations and paid large amounts of money are easily susceptible to late nights, alcohol, and questionable company. Staying in New York, Houston or London won't keep you entirely out of harm's way, but your established norms, traditions, and habits will perhaps help you avoid the worst.

Traders need to approach trading as a career, even though it is measured by the trader and by the company on a day-to-day, trade-to-trade basis. If you work for a good company, learn the business and apply simple rules to your trading, you should make money in the long run. If you can accept that being a trader is not just about how much you made on your last deal or what your bonus will be this year, you can avoid some of the stress involved with making and losing money. Stress, as we discussed, leads to unhealthy activities like drinking and drug-taking. There will always be some stress, though, so that must be dealt with.

Traders deal with stress in various ways. A well-known and very successful trader I worked with swam every day at noon; this was probably inadequate based on some of his behavior in the office, but perhaps without his fifty to a hundred laps a day we would have all been killed or he would be dead from cirrhosis. Many traders I knew were athletes or at least did some kind of regular physical activity. A famous example is Pierre Andurand, the head of one of the last surviving energy hedge funds; Pierre was a champion swimmer in his younger days and now spends many hours a week at the gym training in kick-boxing. I practiced karate for many years, going to the dojo after long hours at the office when I would have preferred sitting down with a beer. Other traders go to the gym regularly during lunch. Physical activity is a great way to eliminate stress and channel unhealthy aggression. Medical science has shown that sitting in front of a computer screen for ten hours a day is more dangerous than smoking or drinking; given that many traders often also drink and smoke, getting up and moving around has great benefits aside from dealing with stress.

There are, as far as I know, no Trader Stress Support Groups. Traders don't admit to being stressed, except in specific, occasional situations and rarely publicly. Being tough, assured, confident, and a Master of the Universe is part of the trader's mystique and persona. Traders won't publicly parade their fears and lack of self-confidence; the other sharks and Alpha males in the market would eviscerate them. A rare counter-example happened to me when I was talking about business travel with a top-level trader. In a rare moment of candor, he admitted something that is apparently common among high-stress, male executives or traders. He had to be extremely careful in his choice of the movies he watched while traveling for work; if he picked something sad, traumatic, or emotional, he found himself crying in business class. Psychologists say this is a sign of pent-up stress which is released in an anonymous setting like the business cabin of an airplane. The passenger lets down his guard because he has no access to phones or Reuters screens. He has perhaps had a drink or two, lowering his emotional inhibitions. He is suffering from different stresses related to being confined on a plane, perhaps a slight fear of flying and possibly fatigue from the journey itself. He is vulnerable. But, rather than admit it, watch Old Yeller, and cry his eyes out when the dog dies, the trader chooses an action movie where the hero and his girlfriend most certainly do not die at the end. He can sip his scotch and keep the lid on his stress for another day!

There are alternatives to sobbing in business class or crying on the shoulders of your colleagues. Many traders seek professional help for both their trading and their mental health. Often these are older traders who fear losing their edge and being replaced by the new generation of twenty-year olds who seemingly need no sleep and know all the functions of their Bloomberg terminal. Sometimes the trader has already started to realize he has a drug (likely cocaine) or alcohol problem which is compounding the rest of the stress. There are psychiatrists and psychologists who make a very good living specializing in Wall Street and City of London clients. But the trader has to make the difficult step of admitting he needs help.

More commonly a trader will seek the help of a trading guru. A trading guru is a trading expert or trading psychologist who is hired to help him with his trading. Most of the time these experts don't give trading advice on what to buy and sell (they either don't know or don't want to give advice to their competitors if they are trading themselves). Instead, they help the trader organize his life, his job, and his trading methods. Most of the techniques are designed to reduce stress, allowing the trader to function closer to peak levels. So a trading guru would recommend having a routine, doing physical activity, having a plan for each trade, following the plan, accepting that losses are part of trading, and aiming for a bigger picture. I would guess that a psychiatrist would recommend the same things but few traders would admit they are seeing a shrink while many would readily boast about how a guru changed their trading for the better.

Trading can also be lonely. Some traders believe that you can't have friends in the market; everyone is an adversary, even your co-workers. I can't see how someone would want to live that way when trading takes up so much of your life. My trading career, for what it was, was buoyed and supported by the friends I made along the way. In fact, some of my best trades were made with my friends, though often that involved losses. By this I mean that I could rely on friends in the market to help me out when I was desperate; yes, they made a profit, but it was moderate and private. Had I been forced into an open market trade, my losses and despair would be public knowledge, an unacceptable outcome for a trader. Additionally, my friends supported my career over the years, often guiding me to better jobs or finding me a job when I needed one. Now, I know there are plenty of traders out there who would prefer being rich to being liked, but having left trading and passed through middle age, I can assure my readers that money is nice, but friends and family are nicer.

The drive to make money is what directs a trader's career, but how that money is made determines what kind of life he has. Traders should ask themselves every day and every time they make a decision about a deal, a questionable transaction, or an after-hours activity, "Is this something I would put in writing and let my parents, wife and kids read, let alone the financial authorities or the police?" If the answer is no for any of those, then there are hard choices to be made. Gary Trudeau wrote that the opposite of wrong is poor, which is wisdom and guidance for many traders, but it is easier to act immorally or illegally if you don't even bother to question your actions in the first place. So, ask yourself, would my mom be proud if she saw me now?

Beyond that, if you still insist on being bad, I can recommend second passports, go-bags, lawyers on retainer, a nest egg of a few hundred thousand dollars for paying off fines or going on the lam, and krav maga lessons for when you end up in prison. As I write these lines, a friend and former colleague is awaiting sentencing for market manipulation. He might end up in jail and, worse, deported upon release. Another former colleague is recently retired and under investigation for bribery and money laundering; he is facing as much as thirty years in prison. There are not many oil traders in the world; I have worked with five who have been arrested and four who have gone or might go to jail![16]

---

[16] I also know many, many oil traders who are fairly honest, decent, and kind. Of course, we all lie since it is part of the job, but not all of us are criminals.

5

Price Risk

At last, we have reached the section of the book that you likely bought it for. Trading is all about making money. Risk management is all about not losing too much of it. Traders are not magicians or seers. They don't get every deal right. They often lose money. When I left trading and went into teaching and consulting, I canvassed a dozen top oil traders across the globe and asked them what were the key characteristics of great traders. With one exception, they all said it was the ability to cut losses. Obviously, if these multi-millionaire and even billionaire traders thought loss cutting was important, it meant they have faced losses on trades. Even the greats like Andy Hall, Marc Rich, John Deuss, Ian Taylor, and Claude Dauphin have had losing trades. What traders like these say separates them from average or weak traders is their ability to accept those losses as a natural part of trading. They can quickly close the position and move on to the next profitable trade. There is no rule that says a trader must win on at least 51% of his trades. All that matters is how much money he has made by the end of the year. If a trader loses money on 99% of his deals but still ends the year with a profit of $20 million, he definitely gets a fat bonus.

In The Black Swan, Nassim Taleb recounts a story of an options trader who loses money every day for up to years at a time. Then, when the stars align and some calamity hits the market, his deep out-of-the-money options pay off phenomenally well, compensating the months or years of losses, and making the trader immensely wealthy in the long run. This options trader can have as many as 300 losing days in a row and then one, big win. The key to his strategy is that the losses are small, small enough that even 300 in a row are not enough to bankrupt the trader or force him to close the position. For those of you who have read The Big Short or seen the movie, this is a similar situation that the hedge fund genius, Dr. Michael Burry, was in; he bled money for a few years before earning $800 million in what was a one-shot payday.

Some great traders are nest-builders, building up their profits weekly in "small" increments. Other traders are home-run hitters who stalk the market throughout the year looking for those few opportunities where they can make half their budget on one big position. What both must do is avoid losing as much as they make. So the "small" trader will aim for, say, $100 profit per trade (these numbers are made up just for illustrative purposes; different traders have different budgets and ideas about what is a lot of or enough money). If he thinks he can get it right half the time, he needs to figure out how much he can lose on wrong trades. Obviously he can't afford to lose $100 on those trades because then he finishes the day, the week, and the year at zero. So he needs to figure out how much he wants to make over the week, how many trades he can reasonably execute in a given market, and calculate how much he can lose on the bad trades and still finish his week on target. If his target is $1280 profit per week and he can't reasonably exit bad trades for anything less than a $20 loss, then he needs to make about 32 trades a week on average. If we assume he loses every other trade, we pair them up so we have one winning trade with a $100 profit and one losing trade with a $20 loss which means each pair of trades makes $80.[1] $80 times 16 equals $1280. Obviously trading is not as neat, tidy, or predictable as this, but the message is that if the trader wants to trade that way, setting his profit target at $100 and closing each deal that hits that level, he needs to set a loss level at $20. If the trader accepts the risk of losing $1000 on a trade while only aiming for $100 profit, he won't last long in the business.

The same logic applies to the home-run hitting trader. He will swing for the fences and hope to make $10,000 on one big trade and expects to do this seven times a year, but he knows he will lose on a certain number of big positions as well. If he wants to earn the same as his "small" trade colleague, he needs to make the same sorts of calculations and make certain he does not lose more than a certain amount on the losing trades. If he gets carried away and loses $40,000 on one position, there might not be enough of his kind of trading opportunities in the market to make up that loss. He might need to start swinging harder and taking more risks just to make his numbers; this is

---

[1] In case anyone thinks he is very clever and suggests that this trader stop at 15 trades and so avoid the final loss of $20 on the 16th trade, I ask you to consider that perhaps the trader starts by losing $20 on the first trade and therefore will make $100 on the 16th trade. Or perhaps he lost on the first 8 trades in a row and then had 8 winning trades. All of these scenarios are statistically unlikely; it would not be that clean and obvious.

often when traders get into trouble and start exceeding limits, lying, cheating, and manipulating.

Logically, then, the first step in managing price risk or trading losses is to set limits on those losses. A trader without a plan is a gambler. A very simple blueprint for trading, which I attribute to Barry Ritholtz, is to have a plan, write it down, and follow it. It's that simple. Decide why you are doing a trade and decide how to enter and how to exit the trade (strategy, profit target, and stop loss, or loss limit). Write the plan down; if it's not written down, it never existed. And then, follow the plan, something which is easier to do when it is in physical form as written in a notebook or in a computer file. Perhaps an ideal trader is one who draws up trading strategies and hands them over to assistants who merely execute them, following the plan exactly.

There are times when trading requires having large positions in place. In order to trade physical oil, it is often necessary to buy and load cargoes of crude oil and products at fixed prices and sell them at some not-yet-determined price (floating price). As we have seen, oil prices can go as high as $147.50 per barrel and as low as minus $40.32, a $178 per barrel range. It is obviously not possible to safely or rationally trade a market where you could lose $100 million on just one cargo when a trader usually deals in several cargoes per month or even several per week. What kind of profit per trade would you need to target if your potential loss on half your deals was $100 million? This is an exaggeration but a few dollars move up or down can cost $4 million on a large cargo of crude oil, the kind of loss that is acceptable only if it is infrequent. Making back that money is difficult and will only bring the trader back to break-even (If a trader loses $4 million on a deal and then earns $4 million on the next deal, he is at zero profit!).

It is clear that traders need to protect themselves from adverse price movements since they can rarely control how much or in which direction the market moves. Even traders who are able to control (squeeze, manipulate, or dominate) local markets such as heavy fuel oil cargo prices in Singapore or gasoline barge prices in Rotterdam over a few weeks or months cannot dictate the direction of Brent or WTI crude oil prices (well, not any more). If the underlying global oil market collapses, fuel oil and gasoline markets will fall as well even if not as far or as fast. Oil trading is as old as modern oil production, and traders have always sought to lock in profits or protect themselves against losses since the early days of crude oil production in the US. For an in-depth look at early crude oil trading, pricing, and hedging, I suggest Adi Imsirovic's book which I previously cited.[2]

---

[2] Trading and Price Discovery for Crude Oils by Adi Imsirovic, Palgrave Macmillan, 2021.

To understand price risk in trading, we need to start with fundamentals. For those of you who know what being long and short are or who have some experience in oil trading, you might wish to skip over this part and go straight to the section on futures contracts. I nonetheless invite all readers to have a look since what you think you know might be different from what you should know. As Mark Twain said, "It ain't what you don't know that gets you into trouble. It's what you know for sure that just ain't so." For those who are fully competent, I invite you to read this section as well in case I made any errors.

5.1   What is Price Risk?

Very simply put, price risk is the possibility of losing money because the market price of oil goes up or down. Markets go up and down. One-day OPEC might announce new production cuts and the price of crude oil might rise by $2 per barrel. The next day China might announce drastic anti-COVID measures[3] and the price might drop by $4 a barrel. Sometimes traders, economists, and analysts can predict the overall trend in a market, which is to say the tendency over a period of days, weeks, or even years that the market will move overall in one direction. Andy Hall famously predicted the long rise of oil prices in the 2000s based on his view on Peak Oil.[4] But not even "God" could have told you that WTI would rise by $1.78 today and drop by $0.46 tomorrow. Nor did he predict the final peak number; he predicted the trend, that the market would rise for many years until something fundamental changed. So Andy Hall did not make money by buying each morning and selling each evening; he bought and bought and bought some more every day over a period of years. Some days he made money, some days he lost a bit back. In the end he made billions (see The Squeeze by Tom Bower for more on this tale), but few traders have the confidence, fortitude, and latitude (trading limits) to do what Andy Hall did at Phibro. In fact, few trading companies these days even let their traders take big, outright positions like Hall did. But that opens up questions we need to answer, such as what is an "outright position?".

In trading we say a trader (or a position) is long, short, or flat (neutral). Since I will be using these terms as we delve into price risk and hedging, it

---

[3] This book was started in 2021 and finished in 2022. Assuming it is still being read years later (and why wouldn't it be), some of you might not recall the COVID Pandemic of 2019–2021.

[4] Peak Oil theory says oil production from known fields hits a maximum level of production and cannot be increased no matter how many wells you drill in it. This original theory was extended to a belief that the world was running out of oil altogether or, in a weaker version of the theory, running out of cheap oil (almost all new production is very expensive).

would be useful to define them clearly. Some definitions of these terms are not directly related to price risk, so let's deal with those first by using some common expressions and defining them.

5.2   One Notion of "Long"

"The Middle East is long crude oil." This means that the Middle Eastern countries produce more crude oil than they can use and need to sell it. The Middle East is a natural exporting zone. While Aramco, Adnoc, and NIOC would certainly like higher oil prices, this statement is not talking about prices but about physical balances in the market. There is too much oil in the Middle East.

"Mercuria is long a cargo a month of Bonny Light." This means that Mercuria has signed a term contract to lift a cargo a month of Bonny Light crude oil from Nigeria over the course of a year. Since most, if not all, term contracts for crude oil do not use fixed prices, this means that Mercuria does not know what price they will pay for each cargo they will lift over the year. Instead, this statement means that the trading company has a contractual obligation to send a vessel to the Bonny Terminal in Nigeria once a month and load a cargo of Bonny Light crude under the terms and conditions of the contract. This creates an obligation for Mercuria to resell the oil since the company does not have crude oil refineries. We don't know what the price of the oil will be, only that Mercuria needs to load cargoes and do something with them.

5.3   One Notion of "Short"

"Europe is short distillates." Since Europe is not a trader or a single company, this is unlikely to refer to prices. Indeed, this statement means that Western Europe has a deficit of gas oil, diesel, and jet fuel. The refining system in Europe does not produce enough of those products to meet European demand. Logically, some other region which is long distillates would ship those products to Europe to balance out the markets.

"She is short a cargo of Jet into the Thames."[5] In this case, the trader has made a sale of a cargo of jet fuel for delivery into the Thames, probably

---

[5] Women are under-represented in the oil trading market. Perhaps it is because women are more rational, sensible, and honest; they are ill-at-ease in what is a Boy's Game. I borrowed this example from a friend and former trader, Suzanne Taylor, who used it in her own teaching material. Had it

into the Isle of Grain for delivery to one of London's airports. In this case, the trader has sold something she does not yet own. She needs to find and buy a cargo of Jet to meet her sales contract commitment. This statement says nothing about how the oil was sold. It might have been done on a fixed price or a "floating price." All we know is that the trader promised to deliver something she doesn't have….yet.

The use of long and short in these sentences says nothing about price risk and won't lead to any conclusions about profits, losses, or hedging. So far we can't tell if any of the traders in our examples will make or lose money if prices go up or down. The following sections will look at how long, short, and flat are used in discussing price risk.

5.4 Long Price Positions

Long positions are created by buying oil at a fixed price. In the simplest terms, imagine you bought a barrel of Brent crude oil at $70 per barrel. Which way would like the market to go? Well, if you are going to be burning it in your furnace, you might not care. But if you are trader, you will likely want to resell the barrel of Brent. Logically, you would like your selling price to be higher than what you paid for the oil. If the market rises to $71, you can sell the oil at the market price and make $1 a barrel profit. Profits make you happy, so a rising market makes you happy if you are long. Now, as childish as this might seem, I have been using the following notation in my teaching to help students understand long and short.

LONG: Prices ↑ = ☺

We read this as follows: If I am long and prices go up, I am happy.

This situation should be clear to most readers since it is common in our everyday lives. We often buy things at fixed prices and keep track of how much they are worth. Most investors buy stock and check the prices every day to see if they are richer. Many of us who own homes might check the real estate market from time to time to see if our house has gained in value. Some collect luxury watches or fine wines which they resell when they have risen in value. I imagine that few of us talk about our houses with friends and remark on how happy we are to be "long" real estate, but that is your position. Let's backtrack and talk about how we get long and when it happens.

---

not been for Suzanne, I would have used "he" and "him" throughout this book, a misogynistic slight on the women in the industry.

5 Price Risk

I started by saying that long positions are created by buying at a fixed price. So buying a cargo of 100,000 barrels of crude oil at $100 and putting it into a storage tank creates a classic long position; the oil will have to be resold at the market price sometime in the future. In this case, the entire cargo was purchased at a single fixed price so we would say the trader is long 100,000 barrels of crude oil. This obviously creates a price risk since if the market falls, the trader will have to sell below $100 per barrel. So, when did the trader get long?

Let's imagine the trader negotiated the deal on 1 June and agreed to the price of $100 per barrel for a CIF delivery into his storage tank on 15 August with options to deliver the cargo to any other terminal in that port. The trader can take delivery into his tank and sell it from there by in-tank transfer (turning over title to the oil in the tank), by pumping it to another tank or terminal (assuming there are connecting pipelines), or by selling it Free on Board (FOB) from his tank. The trader could even resell the cargo CIF (delivered) to another buyer in the port, thereby never taking the oil into his tank.

Let's assume it is the 1st of June, immediately after the deal was concluded. For now, the cargo has not yet loaded and will only arrive in sixty-five days. Perhaps the cargo has not even been produced! The trader has a contract in hand but he has no physical oil and won't get it until 15 August. Does that mean the trader has nothing to worry about until the oil is discharged into his tank? Let's look at his position and his risk.

Suppose the trader decides that since he doesn't have the oil yet, he has no risk. So, what if the market price goes up to $110 on the next day, 2 June? This means the oil he bought for $100 is now worth $110. Can the trader sell the cargo immediately to someone else even though it has not loaded? Certainly, since he bought it under those same terms and conditions, i.e., not yet loaded. He can immediately resell the cargo CIF and pocket $1,000,000 (100,000 bbl x $10 a barrel profit). Making money makes the trader happy. If we check our formula above, we see that being long means being happy when the price rises.

Suppose the price stays at $110 but the trader decides it is bizarre to sell oil he doesn't have yet. He decides to wait until it is delivered into his tank and then sell it. If the market price is still at $110 by the time the oil is delivered and discharged into his tank, he still makes his money; he bought at $100 and can now sell at $110. He was long because he bought oil at a fixed price. He could have made $10 a barrel by selling the oil immediately or by waiting (assuming, as we did, that the price stayed steady at $110 from 2 June until the time of the resale). This means the trader was long from the moment he agreed to the deal, the moment he committed to buying 100,000 bbl of oil at a fixed price. He became long on 1 June at the exact moment or time he agreed to the deal. We would say he was long 100,000 bbl of crude oil at $100 per barrel.

Suppose, on 2 June, the price in the market drops from $100 (the price he agreed to the day before) down to $90 and stays there. Does the trader think, "I have not lost any money yet because I don't have the oil." This makes little sense since the trader will have to sell the oil at some point whether he decides to resell the cargo before it is discharged into his tank or after it is discharged. The price of the oil is set by the market, and if the market is at $90, then that is the value of the cargo. The trader might decide to wait and hope the market goes up, but the market price will remain at $90 for the rest of the year or even forever (this is just an academic exercise so I am playing God and setting the prices), the best price he will ever get is $90. That is the market price for this oil. So the trader has effectively lost $10 a barrel overnight and, in this academic case where we decree the price stays at $90, that loss is set and permanent. If he resells the cargo on 2 June he can get $90 for it even if it has not yet loaded. If he waits to get physical oil in his tank, he can sell it for $90. In both cases he still loses $10. This brings us to the second part of the Long formula:

We said LONG: Prices ↑ = ☺

But in this case prices went down and the trader lost money, making him unhappy. So the second part of the Long Formula goes as follows:

LONG: Prices ↓ = ☹

If I am long and prices go down, I lose money and am unhappy

This should be clear for now. If you buy oil at a fixed price and the market goes up, you are happy because you can sell at a higher price and make money. If you buy at a fixed price and the market goes down, you are unhappy because you sell at a lower price and lose money. In the case of this fixed price purchase, we see that the trader became long as soon as the fixed price was agreed on 1 June. His being long (price risk) was independent of having the physical oil in hand or even of the vessel loading. Indeed, being long in this case is about price, not physical oil.

In Summary, our Long Formula looks like this:

LONG: Prices ↑ = ☺
           Prices ↓ = ☹

5.5 Short Price Positions

Short positions are created by selling oil at a fixed price when you don't have any (or don't have any that you bought at a fixed price). A trader sells a cargo of diesel to a distributor at $600 per metric tonne (MT), but she does not own any oil or at least has not bought any at a fixed price. If the trader owned a cargo (purchased at $590 per MT) and then sold that cargo at $600, we would not say she had shorted the position. Instead, we would say she was flat or had closed the position. Going short (creating a short position) involves selling oil at a fixed price when there is no corresponding long position against it. This is typically more confusing for the layman or new entrants to the market to grasp.

In the normal course of our lives, we don't very often sell things we don't own. We buy cars and resell them. We buy houses and resell them. It is uncommon for people to sell a house first and then buy it back. Imagine explaining to the owners of a house that you have sold their house to another family so they should please now sell it to you so you can fulfill your real estate flipping dream. Often we hear of short sellers in stock markets, but they are often vilified since they are betting on the values of companies dropping, an anti-capitalist sentiment! In any case, it is usually impossible to sell stocks short without having them in your possession in the first place; short sellers are obliged to borrow the stocks in order to sell them. But commodity markets work both ways around with participants going long or going short. Going short a commodity price is not only acceptable, it is usual.

In the case of our diesel trader, what would she like to see happen in the market? She has sold a cargo of diesel for delivery CIF into Lavera, France for delivery during 15–19 July at a fixed price of $600. Since she does not own a cargo of diesel, she needs to go out and buy one. What would she like to see happen in the market. Well, the truism says that traders must buy low and sell high to make money. In this case, she has already sold at $600 so she must try to buy the diesel at a lower price to cover her commitment. If she manages to find a cargo that arrives into Lavera at $590 per MT, she can buy it and make a $10 per MT profit. If the market drops to $500, she can buy a cargo at that price and make a whopping $100 profit. The lower the market goes, the more she should make. She has locked in her sale price and would like to buy as cheaply as possible; the more the market drops, the happier she is.

So now we can start building the Short Formula:

SHORT: Prices ↓ = ☺

When you are short and prices drop, you are happy.

What if the market rises after the trader makes her deal to sell at $600? She will have to go out and buy a cargo (she has a contractual obligation to deliver the cargo) at whatever the market price is. If the market rises to $650, then she will have to pay that much to "cover her short position" (buy a cargo to deliver into her fixed price contract). This represents a hefty $50 per MT loss and she is not happy. So when a trader is short and prices rise, the trader loses money and is unhappy. This gives us the second part of our Short Formula:

SHORT: Prices ↑ = ☹

When you are short and prices go up, you are unhappy because you lose money.

The trader gets short (creates a short position) the moment she agrees to the sale at $600 per MT. The market could rise or fall in the seconds following her saying "Done!".

If we combine the two parts of the Short Formula and re-arrange the order so we start with prices going up (to keep the Long and Short formulae in the same format), we get:

SHORT: Prices ↑ = ☹
        Prices ↓ = ☺

When you are short and prices go up, you are unhappy.
When you are short and prices go down, you are happy.

In both cases, being long and being short, the position was created as soon as a fixed price was set. So it does not matter if you agree to pay $100 for oil that is instantly pumped into your tank or if that oil will be delivered in five years. You become long the instant you agree to the fixed price since you will resell the oil at some point and need the market to rise in order to make a profit. The same is true for being short; the position is created as soon as the fixed price is agreed.

As an aside, if you find that writing Smiley Faces and Frowny Faces in your trading notebook is childish or unprofessional, please use the formulas anyway and change the faces to something else, perhaps a $ instead of the happy face and an "X" instead of the Frowny Face. I often use the following notation which looks scientific and professional: Px ↓ = $ for the second part of the Short Formula, as an example.

5.6 Short and Long with Floating Price Contracts

So far we have talked about buying and selling cargoes of oil using fixed prices. This is, in fact, a fairly uncommon way to trade physical cargoes. Most physical cargoes are traded on what is called a "floating price" basis. So what is a floating price? Well, we have already said that market prices go up and down, so a floating price is a price that is going up and down with the market. It is a price that has not been exactly defined in dollars and cents, a price that has not been fixed. How does a floating price work?

For now, let's avoid too many details about price reporting agencies[6] and benchmarks and simply agree that the price of oil goes up and down. Financial reports on television talk about the price of crude oil and typically refer to WTI futures, though that is not really the international price of oil. We can, for now, simply talk about the market price for oil.

As is clear from the presentations on long and short positions, going long or going short presents a significant financial risk. It takes only a small price movement on a big cargo to create millions in losses. For this reason, many buyers and sellers prefer to set the price of their oil in relation to when they "get their hands on it" rather than at the market price on the day the deal was concluded. So a buyer of a gasoline cargo into New York Harbor might conclude a deal on 20 July to buy 40,000 metric tonnes (MT) of gasoline which will be delivered at the end of August. When the cargo arrives and is discharged, the buyer will load it on trucks and trains and sell it fairly promptly into the retail market. If the buyer agrees a fixed price on 20 July and the market falls, he will sell his gasoline at a loss. He might accept some price risk (a few days on a very small quantity like a one thousand tonnes) but having that much price risk (on 40,000MT) over forty days is too much. Instead, he would like to have a price based on the market price for gasoline when the cargo arrives at his terminal, which is close in time to when he will sell the oil. So he agrees to buy the cargo which will arrive at the end of August and he agrees with the seller that the price will be, for example, the price in the market on the day the cargo finishes discharging. There is still the possibility that the market will drop by the time the buyer loads up his trucks and sells into the market, but the closer the pricing of the cargo is

---

[6] Price Reporting Agencies (PRA) are companies like Platts and Argus that publish daily or weekly reports showing the market price of crude oils and oil products. We do not know where prices will be in the future, but we know what they are once they have been recorded and published by a PRA. PRA's turn floating prices into fixed prices by writing them down and labeling them as "today's price."

to the market timing of his sales by truck, the less risk there is. The market could drop $5 per barrel on any given day or even $10 over a week, but it usually takes a few weeks or months to move the market down by $30 or $50 per barrel. The longer the buyer, in this case, is exposed to the market, the greater the probability that prices will drop far enough to cause him severe financial losses on that cargo.

So far we have not found any solutions to our pricing risk, but we can take a look at some simple ones. In the case of the fixed price purchases and sales, the trader could immediately resell the cargo (or cover his position) at a fixed price. If this is done quasi-instantaneously, there is theoretically no risk from price movements. This is generally impossible to do; traders rarely get the opportunity to instantly conclude a back-to-back trade at a fixed price simply because most cargoes don't trade at fixed prices. The deals would have to line up together with the trader and his colleague sitting side by side. As one confirms the purchase, the other instantly confirms the sale. This might happen from time to time, but it a rarity at best.

The New York Harbor cargo offers a better, more feasible approach to managing the price risk. In this case the buyer tried to line up his purchase price (in terms of when the price was set based on the market) with his sale price by agreeing to set the price of the cargo on a date as near as reasonable to his selling dates for his retail sales. Imagine that instead of discharging the cargo into his tanks and reselling the oil over a week by loading trucks and train cars, the buyer had resold the entire cargo to someone else, either in his tank (In-Tank Transfer[7]) or delivered on the ship (CIF, CFR, or DAP, which are all Incoterms). In that case he could align the pricing of the cargo up without having to set fixed prices for the purchase and for the sale. He could buy the cargo on 20 July as before but the price would be set based on the market level on the day the cargo finishes discharging (what we call COD, completion of discharge). He can then resell the cargo any time before it loads or arrives and set the sale price the same way. So he will buy the cargo using the COD date market price and sell the cargo using the same COD date market price. As an example, if the market price on 20 July was $100, we don't know what it will be on the COD date; we only know that the cargo should contractually arrive at the end of August and complete discharging sometime around there. If the cargo finishes discharging on 28 August, then the purchase price will be whatever the market price is on that date. Let's say

---

[7] In-Tank Transfer is not an Incoterm. It is an industry convention or expression for delivery of oil. The oil is sitting in a tank. The seller passes over the title and risk to the buyer in the tank, so the oil stays where it is.

it's $125. Is this a catastrophe for the buyer because the price went up from $100 to $125 or is it a bonus because now the cargo is worth more?

The buyer will pay $125 for the cargo since that is price determined by the contract. The contract says the price will be the market price on the date of completion of discharge. Whoops! The buyer possibly could have purchased the cargo at $100 if he taken the risk to agree a fixed price on 20 July, the day he concluded the deal. So, is the buyer going to lose $25 because he bought at $125 instead of $100?

The buyer has agreed to resell the cargo based on the market price on the COD (completion of discharge) date. So, his sale price is also $125. Yes, he has paid more for the oil than the market price on 20 July, but he doesn't care. His purchase price is the same as his sale price since they both use the same market price on the same date (I am obviously ignoring margins, premiums, costs, etc., which makes no difference to the principles involved). Of course, if the buyer had agreed to the $100 fixed price when he did the deal and then resold the cargo as described (COD date market price) he would have pocketed $25. But how would he know that the market was going to go up? Suppose the market had dropped instead.

If the buyer had fixed the price at $100 when he did the deal and the market dropped to $75, he would lose $25. But what if he had bought the cargo on the COD date price instead, as we suggested? Would he now get a cheap cargo and make a big profit?

If the price drops to $75 on 28 August, the buyer is not getting a "cheap" cargo because he now has to resell it at $75 to his buyer (he agreed to sell to his buyer at the market price on the COD date). If the price drops, he pays less but he also gets less when he resells the oil. A low price is not "cheap." A high price is not "expensive." Both are simply market prices at that moment in time.

The buyer has agreed two contracts which could be concluded at very different times without creating a price risk. He has agreed to buy a cargo at whatever the market price will be on same date in the future (here we specify that it is the COD date). He later agrees to sell that cargo to someone else using the same date (the COD date). Since he is buying and selling the same oil on the same vessel, there will be only one COD date. The trader has one price and it is the same for his purchase and his sale. We would call this "back-to-back" pricing.

What is the trader's position? We said that he can be long, short, or flat so we need to figure out which one he is. We said that you get long by buying at a fixed price and you get short by selling at a fixed price. The trader in this case did neither so he must be flat; he doesn't care if the market goes up or down. We saw that this was the case when the price rose to $125; the trader paid more, but also received more, $125. And when the price dropped, he paid $75, but then received only $75. If the market had dropped to zero he would have received free oil but then he would have to give it away to his buyer. If the market had gone to one million, he would buy a very high-priced cargo but he would resell it at one million to his buyer. There are no losses or gains to the trader in these scenarios.

At this point, it seems clear that the trader was neither long nor short, but let's use the formulas to make sure. This time, since we are not really sure if the trader is long or short, we can't start on the left-hand side of the formula but need to start on the right-hand side (or rewrite the formulas in a different order):

LONG   **SHORT**
Prices ↑ = ☺   Prices ↑ = ☹
Prices ↓ = ☹   Prices ↓ = ☺

We have gone through all these scenarios with prices going and prices going down and we saw that the trader doesn't make or lose money when prices move. In that case, if the trader doesn't care which way prices go, we say he is flat. So our last formula is as follows:

FLAT FORMULA
Prices ↑ = 😐
Prices ↓ = 😐

If a trader is flat, he doesn't care if prices go up or down. The most basic flat position for a trader is when he has no active deals or positions anywhere, which is unusual except on the first day at a new job.

If this is all new to you or if you still need to think about it for a bit before understanding your positions, I suggest you write down the Smiley Face/Frowny Face formulas on a piece of paper and keep them handy as you read this book. We will be working with positions and hedging over and over, and the formulas will help you make your trading and hedging decisions.

Price risk, being long or being short, can lead to losses. Obviously, price risk can also lead to gains. If a trader buys one million barrels of crude oil, there is at least a fifty-fifty chance that the price will rise the next day. It could even go up by $5 a barrel, making the trader very happy. But it could also fall by the same amount, making the trader unhappy and possibly unemployed. Risk management is not about eliminating profits since profits are the entire reason trading exists. When we talk about hedging price risk, we concentrate on the downside, not the upside. This is important when we look at our formulas. When we think about how to manage our price risk, we need to look at the Frowny Face and deal with that; the Smiley Face will take care of itself as we will see.

I said that fixed price cargo trades are uncommon, but that does not mean they are non-existent. When fixed price trades are made, they create instant and generally large price risks.[8] We looked at an example of a cargo that is priced using the market price at discharge and how that pricing could be used to reduce or even eliminate price risk. One of the interesting points about that cargo is that we don't know what the price will be on the COD date when we conclude the deal. Frankly, as we saw by our analysis, we also don't care what it will be. We only know that it will be a market price that we will examine on some day in the future and use it for our invoicing. Until that day, the market will go up and down and the price will up and down with it, like a cork floating in the sea; sometimes the cork is high on the crest of a wave, sometimes the cork is in the trough. We can't say if the sea level will be high or low on the day the cargo discharges and we can't say if the cork will be high on a crest or low in a trough. The same is true for the market price. We know the market will go up and down but we don't know which way or how far. We will only know the contract price when we get to the agreed date and measure the market together at that time. We call these sorts of prices "floating prices."

A floating price is any price that is not fixed but will be determined (fixed) at some time in the future. Prices must be fixed (turned into real numbers like $73.32 per barrel) at some point in order to prepare an invoice. A floating price deal says that the price is unknown today but will be chosen on a specific date or dates in the future. The dates can be specified or they can somewhat indeterminate. Specified dates would be something like "the price of the oil will be the market price on the 20th of September." Indeterminate dates would be something like "the price of the oil will the market price on the day the vessel completes discharge." We are unlikely to know when the vessel will complete discharge until perhaps a few days before it does, so that COD (Completion of Discharge) dates can be estimated but might shift by just a day or even to many months. If the ship arrives on time and discharges normally, our estimates for a COD would be fairly accurate, the exact date plus or minus one calendar day. If there is some problem like a refinery shutdown, extreme weather, port strike, or a ship blocking the Suez canal, the

---

[8] We can consider a one million barrel cargo as typical for physical crude oil trading and forty thousand metric tonnes as typical for oil product trading. $1 per bbl is about $7.50 per metric tonne (mt or MT) so a $1 per barrel move in oil prices represents a gain or loss of $1 million on a typical crude cargo and $300,000 on a typical product cargo.

cargo might discharge months later than planned. So the COD date, and therefore the market price date, is unknown (indeterminate). Perhaps if all had gone well, the market price on the COD date would have been $500. Instead, the vessel was severely delayed by months and the market price on the COD date was $300.

Floating price contracts are the most common way to buy and sell physical cargoes of crude oil and oil products. Buyers and sellers don't know where prices will be in the future (no one does despite what they tell you) so they usually want to sell at the market price at the time the cargo is physically exchanged. There are many reasons why traders (and here I include traders selling from refineries, traders buying FOB, traders selling delivered, and traders acting as end-users or consumers) don't want to use fixed prices.

The first is the one we have been discussing, very high price risk. We discussed why a trader might not want to deal at fixed prices (see the Smiley and Frowny Faces if you have not yet grasped the concept of profit and loss). Why don't refiners or consumers like fixed prices? Well, some do but they are confronted by traders who won't buy from them or sell to them on fixed prices so there is little they can do but buy and sell on floating prices themselves.

Refiners, like traders, are also interested in making money. Refiners may sell their production weeks to months forward. Indeed many sell their oil on term contracts lasting a year or more. If they lock in the sales of their production at a fixed price, they might find in a month that they have sold their products far too cheaply. You might say, "Well then, why didn't they lock in the crude oil at a fixed price as well? If they did that, they would have a fixed price purchase of their refinery input and fixed price sale of their refinery output. This would lock in the margins!" That sounds very clever, but there are a few flaws. First, the refiner needs to find a supplier who agrees to sell crude oil at a fixed price over the entire year; this is not going to happen in the market. Second, it supposes that if this were even possible, the refining margin was at a level that was high enough for the refiner to want to lock it in. This situation is impractical in the real world.

Instead, the refiner tries to align the market price of his crude purchases with the market prices of his product sales to avoid excessive price risk. This is imperfect on a day-to-day basis since the floating prices of crude and products rarely perfectly align (crude and products move up and down at different rate), but a refinery runs nearly every day for decades. Over many years, the misalignments cancel each other out, and the refinery effectively buys crude and sells products at the same market level over the medium and long term.

The refinery depends on refining margins, not absolute price movements, to make money in the long term.

A consumer is obviously concerned with overpaying. If a consumer locks in a price today for delivery later, he might discover that by the time the cargo arrives, the market has dropped very far. If this consumer is an airline, they might learn that the wonderful deal for a cargo of jet fuel at $750 per MT they concluded three months ago doesn't look so good today when the market is at $500 per MT. Their competitors are buying floating price cargoes based on delivery date pricing, so in the $500 market our airline is paying fifty percent more for fuel than its competition. He can't keep his ticket prices high (to cover his high fuel costs) or travelers will choose another, cheaper carrier. Instead, he has to fill his airplanes at the market price for tickets and eat the loss on his jet fuel. To play it safe and be sure he is competing on a level playing field, the airline will instead choose to buy their fuel on a floating price basis as and when they need it.

I discussed the potential for losses for both refiners and consumers (and of course, we could also talk about crude oil producers but the arguments are all similar), but I did not talk about profits. If there is a price risk there is a potential for loss, but there is also a potential for gain. An airline that locks in its jet fuel purchases for the entire year might be thrilled when prices rise; the airline can sell expensive tickets while paying a cheap price for its fuel. We call this "windfall profits," money made fortuitously or by luck. It is always better to be lucky than wrong in trading, but luck is not something that can be predicted or managed. So an airline trader (fuel buyer) who flips a coin and decides to lock in her fixed price jet fuel for two years might get it right and be lightly rewarded (after all, it was her job to buy jet fuel, and she really just got lucky when the price went up). If the market collapses, the airline will lose millions and face the wrath of its investors and the stock market. Since executives get paid based on the share price, they will be very angry with the trader and fire her. This might be an exaggeration since few large airlines let their trader independently make the decision to lock in prices for the entire year or longer, but it gives you an idea of the problem of trading using fixed prices.

Floating prices are also preferred by lenders, international agencies, regulatory authorities, non-corrupt governments, and honest trading companies. Fixed prices are easy to fiddle with, leading to cheating and corruption. If an international aid agency allocates fifty million dollars to a third-world country for buying oil products, the agency doesn't want the money spent on Ferraris and Swiss ski chalets. The recipient of the funds (the national oil company or the oil ministry, for example) is authorized to make the purchase and then report everything back to the aid agency. It is quite easy for the ministry or the national oil company to meet with a dishonest trader and set the price far above the market level. The trader makes a fortune on the deal and kicks back a portion to the minister or purchasing manager who agrees to the whole arrangement. The aid agency has few ways of knowing if the price is a market price or not. Even ignoring costs and margins built into the price, the aid agency might know exactly when the deal was done. Indeed, if the market has moved from the time of the deal to the time it is reported, they might not even question the deal. Let's look at an example.

Faroffistan receives $50 million from the UN Oil Development Agency for imports of diesel. The managing director of the Faroffistan National Oil Company (FNOC) meets with a trader and they agree to set the price of the diesel at $700 per MT which is $50 per MT above the reasonable market level on the day they do the deal. FNOC sends the contract to the UN a week or so later. The contract shows that the trader will deliver a cargo in two months time at $750. By the time the UN has received the contract and seen the price, the market price has risen to $775 per MT, and the UN sends a congratulatory email to FNOC on their savvy and their excellent negotiating skills. When the cargo finally loads, the market price is $850 per MT and no one would dream of suggesting that the deal is somehow corrupt. Given the way markets move up and down, this scenario could even play out between a deal done in the morning and reported in the afternoon, assuming the market rose or dropped enough.

Imagine a new head of purchasing at FNOC who is honest and competent. Instead of the managing director handling the purchase, the task is given to the new head of purchasing. He spends a few days negotiating with a trader and finally does a great deal. He gets the trader to agree to a fixed price which works out to be cheaper than what the market might expect (perhaps the trader is desperate to sell a cargo, wants to establish a commercial relationship with FNOC, or simply made a mistake). He prepares the contract and sends it to the managing director for signature. The MD is out of the office and only returns two days later whereupon he finds the contract on his desk. He reads it and checks the price on the market. Lo and behold, he discovers that the head of purchasing paid $675 for a cargo but the market today is only $600, having dropped by $100 since the deal was concluded. Obviously, in his mind, the head of purchasing is corrupt and has agreed to an over-the-market price in return for a kickback (bribe). Depending on how FNOC is run, one of two things might happen: the MD might fire the head of purchasing and refuse to sign the contract or he might sign it and demand that the head of purchasing give him the lion's share of the kickback. If the opposition party hears of this deal, they will demand the resignation of the MD and the Minister of Natural Resources.

While I picked a fictional third-world country, the same logic and schemes apply to the developed world. Nigeria and Indonesia might be famous for everyday corruption, but a European or US buyer would be tempted to do the same thing. Using fixed prices in contracts, especially term contracts lasting a year or more, opens up the door to easier corruption. For this reason and the others we talked about (price risk), most market participants prefer to use floating prices. The price of the oil will be set by the market when it is delivered whether the market goes up or down.

We talked about COD (completion of discharge) pricing which sets the contract price at the end of the voyage after the cargo is off the ship. We can also use arrival at destination pricing which we would call NOR pricing (Notice of Readiness, the official declaration from a vessel that it has arrived at a port and is ready to carry out operations, in this case discharge the cargo).[9] However, the most common way to use floating prices is to set the price of a cargo based on the market prices around the time the cargo is loaded onto the vessel. This is called a bill of lading pricing or B/L pricing. The bill of lading is the document that evidences the existence of the cargo and that it has been loaded on board a certain vessel on a certain date. For a producer or refiner, the bill of lading date usually means the day the cargo is formally and physically put into the hands of the FOB buyer and the day the vessel sails away with the cargo. Since the producer or refiner won't see that oil again and doesn't care about when it will be ultimately resold, they want to link their pricing to the day it was handed over, the bill of lading date.

When we talked about market prices on certain days (e.g., the Completion of Discharge date or Bill of Lading date), we did not discuss any details about what those prices are or where they are found. For now, we will simply refer to the "market prices on the day." Later, as we talk about understanding the prices we use in trading, we will look into the prices which are published on futures screens and in market reports such as Platts and Argus. Market prices are not, however, sacrosanct and perfect prices determined by the Invisible Hand and which represent the free and fair market value of the oil in question. Markets are made of people and often just a few people when it comes to making oil prices. Markets are made up of human beings with all their flaws and features.

---

[9] The contract will often stipulate that the NOR must fall within the agreed delivery period. If the vessel is early or late, the NOR date, and therefore pricing dates, will be deemed to have taken place on an agreed date (e.g., the NOR is deemed to have been tendered on the final day of the delivery range). This can also be applied to Bill of Lading pricing; if the vessel arrives after the delivery dates, the seller may require a "deemed" B/L date, typically the last day of the delivery range.

In markets like the Platts Singapore jet fuel market[10] (Platts is the main price reporting agency for crude oil and oil products. Platts prices are used to buy and sell most of the oil and oil products traded across the globe), there are a handful of companies and perhaps a dozen traders who participate in the pricing activity that Platts uses to determine the price of jet fuel on any given day. This is true for almost all the Platts markets and prices around the globe; each market has a few to a couple of dozen traders who are active in setting the prices. To be clear, there are thousands of oil traders across the globe, but most of them do not participate in the specific mechanism called the Platts Window (or Market on Close)[11] which sets the daily prices for crude oil and oil products. A market price for jet fuel (or, as they call it there, kerosene) in Singapore cannot be set at a random price by those dozen traders unless they are all colluding; the prices might move up or down but are unlikely to move to ridiculous levels relative to, say, Brent crude oil. Of course, your definition of "ridiculous" might depend on whether or not you are happy or hurt by the way Singapore jet fuel prices move.

If Brent crude oil drops by $20 per barrel, it would be somewhat surprising to see jet fuel prices rise by $20 on the same day, though it is not inconceivable (a more likely event would be Brent rising by $20 a barrel and jet fuel going up by $40 per barrel, something that might happen in the event of a war in the Arab/Persian Gulf). Assuming there is no information in the market specific to jet fuel supply and demand, we would expect jet fuel prices to rise and fall almost in lock-step with the changes in crude oil prices. So traders trying to manipulate prices would be unlikely to get jet fuel prices up by $100 per barrel if crude drops by $10 per barrel. That said, they could likely get jet fuel prices to go up or down by $2 even if crude oil prices don't change.

But it takes money and resources to manipulate markets. If a trader wants the prices in Singapore to rise over the entire month, he needs to make the prices higher every working day from four pm to four-thirty pm by buying cargoes and swaps during the Platts Window. It is far easier to do this on just one day rather than twenty or twenty-two days (a calendar month typically has about that many working days). If a trader wants the market prices higher,

---

[10] Jet fuel in Singapore is called Kerosene in Platts. This is because a large portion of Asian jet fuel consumption is really as kerosene for lighting, heating, and cooking. Many countries have special specifications for their production and imports which they call Dual Purpose Kerosene (DPK), which is a kero-type product that meets both jet fuel specification and domestic kerosene specifications.

[11] Platts reports daily prices for crude and products by essentially taking a snapshot of the market at 4:30 pm in each of the main markets: Singapore, London, and NY. The prices looked at by Platts are those which are publicly traded in a special market called the Platts Window. It doesn't matter where the market was in the morning; the day's published prices are calculated based on where the prices are at the close of the market (MOC or Market on Close) at 4:30 pm.

he needs to buy oil at higher prices. This requires financing and creates many risks. The oil will have to be loaded, shipped, and resold. Just buying one cargo a day in the Singapore market means ending up with 20 cargoes or about 4.8 million barrels of jet fuel worth half a billion dollars or more.

So a trader might get jet fuel prices to spike on one day and then let them return to normal market levels for the rest of the month. Let's assume a buyer agrees to purchase a cargo from a trader based on the market price on the bill of lading date. It is possible that the trader is long jet fuel and (checking our Smiley Faces) we know he would like the market to go up. It is possible and relatively easy for the trader to manipulate the market for just that one day and drive the prices up, making them higher than the normal market level.

The buyer ends up paying a price that is above the market price that prevailed before the pricing date and after the pricing date. For example, the buyer agrees to pay the market price for the jet fuel on the day loading is completed (the B/L date). The buyer watches the market and it is steady at $700 per MT until the day his cargo finishes loading. Suddenly, the market price spikes to $750 for no reason other than his supplier (the trader) is driving the price up during the Platts Window (frankly, many buyers won't even understand how the Window works so they won't catch on to the trader's games). The next day the market drops right back down to $700. The buyer ends up paying $750 for his cargo and is very unhappy and convinced it was all just bad luck; his B/L date just coincided with a "random" rise in jet fuel prices.

Market manipulation aside, it is possible for prices to rise or fall dramatically in one day, even for a few minutes. Sharp price spikes and brief collapses occur regularly without intentional manipulation or fraud. Markets are driven by information, sometimes in the form of facts and often in the form of rumors or guesses. If there is a market rumor that Saudi and Iranian warships have started firing on each other and war has been declared, it might not matter if this story is quickly denied and disproved if the news came out at 4:25 pm in Singapore just as the daily market prices were being determined by Platts. The market price for jet will jump to $900 per MT for ten minutes until a new Reuters headline explains it was really just fireworks being set off by a luxury yacht cruising through the Straits of Hormuz. At 4:35 it is too late to change the prices for the day. Platts lets the market decide what the price is and will report the market at 4:30 pm. Very often market prices move because of rumors and misreporting. Platts cannot go back and change prices because we learn later that the rumors of war were unfounded or that talk of OPEC quota increases was misinterpreted. Of course, Platts might correct prices if it can be shown that a fake story was planted in order to fraudulently manipulate the market. It is not clear just how far back Platts would go, but it is clear that Platts rarely changes prices unless there is an error in their calculation or printing.[12]

A buyer or seller who puts all his eggs in one day's basket risks seeing his price manipulated intentionally or unintentionally. In any case he risks a spike or a one-day collapse. To avoid this, most deals use more than one day to set the prices. For example, instead of using the Bill of Lading date price, the contract says to use a five day average of the two days before the B/L date, on the B/L date, and the two days following the B/L date. Even if there is a price spike or collapse in one day, it only affects one-fifth of the cargo since it concerns only one-fifth of the price. So in the case of a cargo buyer who is loading 50,000 MT, if she chooses to set the price based on the market price on the B/L date, she might "overpay" by $50 on 50,000 MT and lose $2.5 million on the cargo. If she agrees to price to cargo over five days, that price spike still takes place but the $50 is averaged over five days, diluted if you like, and ends up costing her only $500,000.

I often tell my clients or training course participants that they should probably move to an average of the month pricing for their oil purchases and sales. This makes perfect sense and smooths out the risk over the entire month. It also eliminates most of the worries associated with knowing when trigger dates will occur for floating prices. (By trigger dates I am referring to things like the Bill of Lading or Completion of Discharge dates. These dates shift when there are changes in shipping operations.) If someone is buying or selling four or more cargoes a month and they are evenly spread across the month, then using a three or five day pricing around the B/L date also makes sense since having so many cargoes means you are buying on a monthly average or close enough. There is nothing magical about buying on monthly average pricing (the price of the cargo would not be based on the market level on the day it loads, for example, but on the average market level over the entire month of loading or delivery), but the derivatives market (for hedging and speculating) is based on monthly average pricing. Lining up your physical pricing with the most common, liquid derivatives makes a lot of sense for reasons we will discuss later.

---

[12] In the recent case where a trader admitted to manipulating prices in the US fuel oil market, Platts reported the manipulated prices (that was the whole point of the manipulation). The trader admitted to doing this over a ten year period between 2011 and 2019 in the US Gulf Coast and from 2012 to 2016 in the Los Angeles market. Platts denies that the manipulation worked or that their prices don't reflect market prices. Consequently, Platts has not amended any of its prices for the US Gulf Coat or Los Angeles as far as I know. The principle is that manipulated prices are still market prices because they were used for real deals.

So, do floating price contracts, whether they are monthly averages or one-day averages, eliminate price risk? The short answer is "no." The longer answer involves understanding what happens when you agree to buy or sell oil using a floating price. Since I have already introduced Platts, I will start referring to it when talking about floating prices since it is, as I mentioned, the most important source of market prices for setting invoices. I will explain how Platts and the Platts Window work in more detail later but for now it is enough to say that Platts reports market prices for oil and oil products and traders use these prices to exchange crude oil and oil products around the world. If we want to know the market price for gasoline cargoes in Singapore today as an example, the only reliable, reputable, and accepted source of prices is Platts. I should mention Argus as well, a competitor who carries out the same role but is less used for the most part. If you talk to someone in the market and ask them what the price of Rotterdam diesel barges was yesterday, they will certainly consult Platts for the answer. This might not be true for all products or all crudes; some markets, such as VGO[13] and Sour Crude in the US Gulf Coast, use Argus. So with no offense to Argus, I will use Platts when referring to published market prices.

Floating price deals have price formulas which may contain premiums or discounts but which also must necessarily refer to some source of market prices. A typical example would be a contract for the FOB purchase of a cargo of high sulfur fuel oil from a refinery in Rotterdam. The price clause might read:

Price: the average of five quotations of the mean of Platts European MarketScan price for Barges 3.5 PCT under the heading FOB Rotterdam plus a premium of $1 per metric tonne. The average price shall be based on the five quotations centered on the bill of lading date of the cargo (two before, the bill of lading date and two after).[14]

If we assume the vessel is going to load in a few weeks and we estimate the bill of lading date will fall on a Wednesday, we assume the price of the cargo will be based on the average of the mean prices published by Platts on Monday, Tuesday, Wednesday, Thursday, and Friday. The mean price in this

---

[13] VGO is vacuum gas oil which is produced by a vacuum distillation unit. It is a dirty product which is further refined in a cracker and turned into gasoline or diesel fuel.

[14] Mean of Platts means the average of the high and low quotations published by Platts. In the past, a single quotation covered more than one grade of product so there would be a low price and a high price. To avoid spikes or discrepancies, most deals used the average of the two. Today, Platts prices represent one specific quality, cargo size, and delivery so the high and low quotes are nearly identical. Platts should probably just publish one price to simplify things. Contrary to what some have argued with me, you can calculate the Mean price if there is only one price!

case ("Mean of Platts") is the average of the high and low prices published by Platts for barges (or whatever crude or product we are talking about). The average of the five prices is calculated and the premium is added on top. Until Platts publishes the prices or at least until 4:30 pm London time on the Monday of the loading week, we don't know how much our cargo will cost; the price is floating and could go up or down. Only when Platts assesses the market at 4:30 will know our prices. Let's look at an example:

Let's assume, as we said, that the vessel completes loading on Wednesday and we have agreed on pricing as we noted above. Each day Platts will assess the market and eventually send out their official report a few hours later. It is crucial to note that even if you receive your copy of Platts by email only the following morning, the price was assessed by Platts at 4:30 pm on the date marked on the copy of the Platts report. Let's assign some prices (Table 5.1):

As we discussed earlier when talking about setting the price at the market level on the day the vessel completes discharge, we can evaluate our risk in this case when we have five days pricing. The mathematical principles are the same. Under the Completion of Discharge pricing we saw that we had no price risk (we were neither long nor short) until the day the cargo was priced; once the cargo was assigned a price, risk was created. A floating price floats only until the time the contract says it must be pinned down. At that point, a floating price turns into a fixed price and we can start using our Long and Short formulas to see what kind of risk we have. Under the COD pricing we had only one price on one day and so became long the entire cargo on that day. Under this new five day average pricing we need to examine our risk again to understand what our position is under a five day average pricing.

When I ask students if there is a position at the end of the day on Tuesday, they say there is not because the cargo does not have a final fixed price. If we use a 50,000 MT cargo in this example, many of my students would say that there is no position (the trader is flat) until 4:30 on Friday when the final

Table 5.1 Example of Platts prices and final contract price for a floating price fuel oil deal

Mean of Platts 3.5 PCT Barges	
Monday	$430/Mt
Tuesday	$420/Mt
Wednesday	$410/Mt
Thursday	$400/Mt
Friday	$390/Mt
Average price: $410/Mt (sum of the above prices divided by five days)	
Premium: $1 per Mt	
Invoice Price: $411 per Mt	

Platts price is known and the five day average (or invoice price) can be fully calculated. Is this correct or not?

Using a five day average of the prices I listed above, we saw that the final invoice price would be $411/MT (Platts five day average of $410 plus a $1 premium). At the end of the week the trader is obviously long 50,000 MT at $411.

What if we changed the deal and, instead of having the trader buy 50,000 MT from one person using the five day average price, he buys 10,000 MT each from five different suppliers. Supplier one sells him 10,000 pricing on Monday (using Monday's Platts price plus $1). Supplier two sells him 10,000 MT pricing on Tuesday. And so on through the week with separate 10,000 MT contracts pricing on each remaining day of the week. In this case there would be five separate invoices with the prices and volumes as follows (Table 5.2):

Since the cargoes have been loaded together and commingled on the vessel, we can consider that the trader now has a cargo of 50,000 MT of fuel oil. What is the cost of that 50,000 MT? Well, clearly it is calculated by taking the weighted average of each contract. In this case we multiply 10,000 times $431 and add that to 10,000 MT times $421, etc. This works out to $20,550,000. If we divide that by the total amount of fuel oil, we get an average price of $411 per MT. This is the very same price we calculated when using the five day average. So that means buying a whole cargo priced on the average of five days is the same as buying five equal cargoes (one-fifth each of the big cargo) pricing on each of the five days. What does this tell us?

In the case of buying five individual cargoes each pricing separately on Monday, Tuesday, etc., we can easily figure out the position on each day. At 4:30 on Monday, when Platts has assessed the market price for the day, we have a good idea (or should have one if we are good traders) what that day's price is. But even if we don't know what the Platts price is, we should realize that the trader has a position. He now owns 10,000 mt at $431 per mt. He is the proud owner of a small fixed price cargo. We can rely on the definition of being long and see that he is long because he bought oil at a fixed price,

Table 5.2 Creating a long position with average pricing over five days

Monday	10,000 Mt bought at $431/ MT (Platts + $1 per MT)
Tuesday	10,000 MT bought at $421
Wednesday	10,000 MT bought at $411
Thursday	10,000 MT bought at $401
Friday	10,000 MT bought at $391

or we can work out the Smiley Face and Frowny Face and figure out if the trader is long or short. Well, he owns oil that he paid $431 for. Would he like the market to go up so he can sell it higher and make money? Yes, of course, so let's check our formulas for that scenario. We readily see that if he is happy when the market goes up, he is long. So in the case of five separate contracts, each pricing on each different day of the week, we get long 10,000 mt of fuel oil every day. So on Monday at 4:30 we are long 10kt. On Tuesday we add another 10 kt and so are long 20 kt at 4:30 on Tuesday. And so on until Friday at 4:30 when we add the last 10 kt and become long the entire 50,000 MT.

We can see from this exercise that buying a cargo over the average of five days creates the same price risk as buying one-fifth of the cargo each day over that same period. Consequently, we can say that even under the five day average pricing, even when we don't know the final price until the end of the day on Friday, we are getting long 10,000 mt every day of the week. Knowing one-fifth of your final price is the same as knowing the fixed price for one-fifth of your cargo. So a floating price contract starts creating price risk as soon as the pricing dates in the contract start coming into effect.

If you don't believe this, please run through the exercise again. Then imagine that the oil is resold the following week at a market price of $391 per mt. In one case, the trader sells five separate cargoes of 10,000 mt each to five different buyers but all at a fixed price of $391. In the second case he sells the full 50,000 mt to one buyer at $391. The profit and loss (P&L) will be the same for both cases, a one million dollar loss.

This concept is the key to effective hedging. Price risk is created as and when any part of the cargo has a fixed price or when any part of the final price has been fixed (e.g., one price out of five is already known). This means the trader gets long each day of pricing which has implications for how he needs to protect himself (how he needs to hedge). Here is a presentation of how the trader's position changes and grows over the five day pricing period (Table 5.3):

Table 5.3 Building a position over a five day average pricing for 50,000 mt of fuel oil

	Pricing: Five day Platts average price on 50,000 mt				
	Monday	Tuesday	Wednesday	Thursday	Friday
Platts Price in $/MT	$430	$420	$410	$400	$390
New Position in MT*	+10,000	+10,000	+10,000	+10,000	+10,000
Position at End of Day	10,000	20,000	30,000	40,000	50,000

*10,000 mt is purchased at a fixed price every day. In trading parlance, we would talk about "new length," "adding length," or "getting longer" each day

At the end of the five day period (the moment the final market price is determined, which is the case of Platts in this example would be at 4:30 pm on Friday but could be different for other market prices), the trader is long 50,000 mt of fuel oil at $411 per mt (the average price over the five days). The trader now has a few options for selling the cargo. He can sell it at the market price of $391 and lock in a one million dollar loss (he is long at $411 and can sell at $391 so he loses $20 per mt on 50,000 mt), or he can sell it at a floating price, say for the last week of the month, dates which coincide with when the vessel arrives at the discharge port. Does selling on a floating price make any difference?

Let's assume the vessel will arrive at the discharge port as planned and the pricing dates for the sale will be the Platts prices for fuel oil from 25 to 29th of the month. Since the trader doesn't know what the price of fuel oil (or crude oil) will be in two weeks, he doesn't know how much he will get for his cargo, but he hopes it's better than what he would get by selling at today's price of $391. The vessel sails for about two weeks and the trader starts checking his position and his P&L. Here is what he sees.

The first thing the trader realizes is that selling his 50,000 mt over a five day average is the same as selling five 10,000 mt cargoes each pricing on one day (10,000 mt sold on 25th using the Platts price of that day, 10,000 mt sold on 26th using the Platts price of that day, and so on). He quickly checks his Long and Short formulas, runs a simulation of his risk, and realizes that the position is going to change every day even if he does not yet have all five Platts prices; it is just like the purchase pricing over a five day average. Here is the table of his positions over the week of 25th to 29th showing his position at the end of the day on 25th (Table 5.4):

The trader realizes that at the end of each day of the week his position will get smaller and smaller until it disappears at the end of the day on Friday. Here is the table filled out (Table 5.5):

Table 5.4 Five day average pricing table at the end of the first pricing day

	Pricing: Five day Platts average price on 50,000 mt				
	25th	26th	27th	28th	29th
Position at Start of Day	Long 50 kt				
Change of Position on Day	−10,000*				
Position at the End of Day	40,000				

*The negative sign means the trader is selling the fuel oil; the long position is being reduced by 10 kt. If we write that the position is −40,000 mt, this would mean the trader is short 40 kt

Table 5.5 Five day average pricing table at the end of the last pricing day

	Pricing: Five day Platts average price on 50,000 mt					
	25th	26th	27th	28th	29th
Position at Start of Day	50,000	40,000	30,000	20,000	10,000
Change of Position on Day	−10,000	−10,000	−10,000	−10,000	−10,000
Position at the End of Day	40,000	30,000	20,000	10,000	0

We were primarily interested in the changes in the position and so did not talk about price and P&L under this scenario. Did the trader make money selling this way? Did he lose more instead? Unless we make up some prices, we can't know. We certainly could not know back when he made the decision to sell his cargo at a floating price. All we know is that the market might go up and it might go down. Yet, there is an important lesson here.

Suppose the market had gone up over the month and the average price from 25 to 29th was $421/mt. The trader avoided a one million dollar loss and turned it into a $500,000 profit. This was done purely by luck; the trader flipped a coin and chose to wait and see what the market did. If his manager lets him trade this way (allowing him to go long 50 kt), then the trader will get a bonus, but only if he can string together a long enough streak of wins to make a large profit at the end of the year. If the trader needs to make five million dollars in order to get a bonus (this is a typical minimum budget), then he must be lucky on ten trades. Flipping a coin ten times in a row and getting heads each time has a probability of 0.1%. (Once every 1024 attempts. So if you flip a coin ten times and write down the results, then do that again and again until you have done this 1024 times, you should see a list of ten heads in a row just once.)

Now, the trader does not have to start his trading year and immediately make ten winning deals in a row and then stop until the next year. Winning ten times in a row is too unlikely to be a reliable trading system. The trader might think that he only has to have ten more winning trades than losing trades. So if he does one hundred deals over the year, he just needs to have 55 winners and 45 losers. If he does 1000 trades, he needs to have 505 winners and 495 losers. Suddenly this seems reasonable. Except that if this is random luck; there is no reason to believe he won't finish the year with 500 wins and 500 losses. The more trades he does, the more likely he is to finish at break-even if it is just "50–50" trading.

The sad truth is that, if the trader relies on luck and prayers to make up his P&L, he has an equal chance of losing or winning. He might start with a string of six losing trades in a row and have a P&L at −$3 million. If the trader does only fifty deals over the year, the odds of having at least six losers in a row is close to 30%. There is a nearly 2% chance of losing ten deals in a row and having a –$5 million P&L. While making three or five million this way might get you a bonus, losing the same amount is likely to get you fired. Additionally, in these examples, we assumed the loss was only $10 per mt. What if the market collapses by $100 per mt the week before the vessel arrives at the discharge port. Suddenly the loss is $5 million on just one cargo!

It is clear that using floating prices is not a magical solution to price risk unless we use them wisely. In the example where the trader was importing a cargo of gasoline into New York Harbor, the trader bought and sold the cargo based on the same market price on the Completion of Delivery (COD) date. The two contracts (buy and sell) were aligned so that the pricing was "back-to-back" and the trader did not care which way the prices went. So, in the case of our fuel oil cargo, the trader could have resold the cargo using the same Platts pricing dates that were used for the purchase. He would have paid $411 for the cargo and resold it at $411. The drop in the market would not bother him at all since he was "flat" the entire time.

Trading does not always work this way. Traders often cannot get back-to-back pricing on their cargoes and often don't even want it. Traders make money by creating risk! By choosing different pricing periods and mechanisms, traders hope to make profits. Of course, this does not mean they close their eyes, say a prayer, and hope the market moves the way they want. I have spent over thirty years in the oil industry, and while I have met many deeply religious people, I cannot recall ever meeting an oil trader who was a priest, a rabbi, an imam, or a shaman; God may answer some prayers but I suspect that a trader's prayers for more money are far down his list.

Earlier I mentioned that there was a lesson here and a difference between selling straight away at $391 or waiting for what the market might do. The lesson is the huge loss of $5 million on the cargo. Playing Russian roulette with one bullet is already risky, but playing with three is insane. The lesson here is the trader should have sold the cargo at $391 immediately, taken his $500,000 loss, and moved on. Any upside (profit) was unlikely since he already had to dig his way out of that half a million dollar hole and only then start to make money. His downside was potentially huge and job-threatening. Traders like Nick Leeson know all about hope and prayers; Lesson started with very small losses, hoped they would go away, and watched them balloon into $1.4 billion. Had Leeson taken his $2 million loss at the start, he would have possibly been fired but certainly not sent to jail, and Barings Bank would have survived a little while longer. A trader should cut or hedge his price risk when it arises.

6

Hedging Price Risk

6.1 What is a Hedge?

Now that we know what price risk is and how it comes about, we can start looking into how to manage it or eliminate it. Managing, reducing, or eliminating price risk is called hedging. Investopedia (a financial website) tells us that "a hedge is an investment that is made with the intention of reducing the risk of adverse price movements in an asset. Normally, a hedge consists of taking an offsetting or opposite position in a related security." The word itself has origins in the same word that is used to describe a living or artificial fence; today we use hedge in landscaping only for the living kind of fence (a line of bushes that act as a barrier of sorts). A hedge made of thorny plants with close-knit branches can keep sheep or horses from passing through and escaping (losing livestock creates a loss for the farmer). So a hedge on a position is a fence around the position which limits losses.

Investopedia's definition is pretty good. It is at least understandable to most readers, especially those who have gotten this far in the book. Investopedia's definition is aimed at those buying and selling stocks and bonds for the most part so it mentions "investment" and "related security." If we rewrite this definition for oil trading we get the following:

> A hedge is a trade or position that is made with the intention of reducing the risk of adverse price movements. Normally a hedge would consist of taking an

Supplementary Information The online version contains a free hedging workbook with detailed answers available at https://doi.org/10.1007/978-3-031-44465-4_6.

offsetting or opposite position in a related derivative such as a futures contract or a swap.

If we have a position that creates risk (we are long or short), we enter into a new position that offsets that risk. The obvious and most simple solution is to resell the entire position. If you own oil at a fixed price, resell that oil. So if you buy a cargo of 50,000 mt of fuel oil at $400, immediately sell it back-to-back at $400. This certainly eliminates risk, but it also makes trading difficult and only marginally profitable. Traders make money by being clever. That often means buying a cargo from one place and time and delivering it to a different place and time. By different time, I obviously don't mean shipping 30,000 mt of unleaded gasoline to fifteenth-century Germany. This means having different pricing dates, for example buying a cargo whose price is set around the bill of lading date and reselling that cargo using the prices around the delivery date a month later. Additionally, if the trader has promised a cargo to a customer (he is short a cargo to that buyer), he can't very well sell off all his oil; he still needs to bring a cargo to this buyer. Instead, the trader needs to find a way to protect himself against "adverse price movements" without getting rid of his physical cargo.

Indeed, the cargo is not to blame for the risk. The cargo is just a bunch of hydrocarbons being sloshed about in an oil tanker. The trader is worried about prices, not molecules. We need to go back to our Smiley Faces and Frowny Faces to see what he cares about and what that implies for hedging.

6.2 Basic Principles of Hedging

Let's take the easiest case first, a trader who owns 100,000 barrels of crude oil sitting in his storage tank. The oil has been priced and paid for. It is now fixed price oil. The trader is obviously long. The trader is not panicking about profits; she is worried about losses. At some point in the future she will have to sell that oil; if the price is lower, she loses money. She could sell it now, but perhaps she has made a deal to sell this particular oil to a customer for delivery in one month with pricing based on the market when it is delivered. She can't sell this oil now unless she is certain she can buy more later. If she can't be sure of that or if that is too difficult, she needs to figure out how to protect herself from falling prices. She needs to hedge.

When we talk about hedging we are concerned with "adverse" price changes and reducing the risk of losses. That means we need to do something about the Frowny Faces. Let's look at our formula.

LONG: Prices ↑ = ☺
       Prices ↓ = ☹

We know that a long trader is worried about prices going down so we need to do something about the Frowny Face. We don't want to eliminate the Smiley Face, but that might be out of our control as we will see later. First, let's deal with the Frown. If we are long, we can't just decide that prices won't go down or call Platts and bribe them to raise prices or at least keep them stable. We need something realistic and legal. We saw that having pricing for our purchase and for our sale on the same day eliminates price risk; we balanced out our purchase with a sale. This back-to-back pricing really means that the risk created by buying (pricing in) oil each day was offset by selling (pricing out) oil each day. So the risk created by a fixed price purchase is offset by a corresponding fixed price sale.

Unfortunately, the pricing days are not the same in this case; the trader is already long the oil (she owns it at a fixed price) and the selling prices won't be known for about a month. If the market drops by the time she starts seeing the prices that apply to his sale, she will lose money. She definitely has a Frown to worry about. So in order to neutralize the Frown, she needs to do something similar to what we did with our back-to-back trade; she needs to do something that makes her happy if prices drop. The Frowny Face needs to be neutralized or offset by a Smiley Face.

As we look through our formulas we see that her long position means a Frown when prices go down. So we look and try to find a Smiley when prices go down. All we need to do is find something that compensates the trader if the price of our oil drops. Lo and behold, our diagrams tell us that being short makes us happy when prices go down. A short position can offset or balance out a long position. In order to hedge her long position, the trader needs to create a corresponding short position. When she combines a long position with an equal and opposite short position, she gets a flat position. When the position is flat, she doesn't care if the market goes up or down. Let's look at the 100,000 bbl of crude oil sitting in the trader's tank.

The trader is long 100k bbl. She has sold the oil at a floating price which is not yet known. If the market price drops she loses money. So she needs to find a different position that pays her back if the price drops, a deal which makes money when the price drops. Well, from our formula we know this means selling something at a fixed price.[1] Since this is a hedge and the trader can't

---

[1] Check your Faces. From the right side, find a Smiley Face when the market drops. Then see which position that is. And then figure out how you get that position.

simply resell her cargo (she will be delivering it to her buyer), she needs to sell something else at a fixed price. Our definition of a hedge says she should most likely sell a swap or futures contracts, but there are other ways to hedge. What most concerns the trader is protecting her price, so she needs to find something that makes her money for every penny the price of the crude oil drops.

A simple way for the trader to hedge and avoid trading derivatives (I have mentioned "derivatives" but we have not defined what they are or how they work, so let's start with something more basic.), would be to take an opposite position on a different physical cargo of oil. Since the trader is long in the first place, she would need to sell 100,000 bbl of crude oil to someone else at a fixed price. These are two different trades so the trader still keeps the original oil in her tank. Let's look at how this would work.

The trader is long 100,000 bbl which will be priced based on Platts prices for the following month. The trader paid $70 for the oil. If next month's average price is lower than $70, the trader loses money. Say the market drops by $10 per barrel, the contractual sale price will be $60, so the trader will lose $10 per barrel, or $1 million dollars.

To hedge this position, the trader sells a different cargo of 100,000 bbl of crude oil to another buyer in a different place at $70. The trader doesn't own any other oil and cannot use her oil in tank to cover this new commitment. She needs to buy another cargo sometime next month and deliver it to this new buyer. She has created a short position. She is short a physical cargo of oil. She is also short that cargo at $70. If the market next month drops below $70, she will be able to buy a cargo cheaper than her sales price and make a profit.

Let's say the market drops to $65 per bbl and stays there for the rest of the month and the following month. The original long position in tank (100 k bbl) is delivered to the first buyer at $65 per bbl (Platts average for the month) so the trader loses $5 per barrel on the deal: she bought the oil at $70 and sold it on a floating price which turned out to be $65. But the trader also needs to buy physical oil for her other, short trade. She can now buy a cargo of crude oil in the market at $65 and deliver to her other buyer at $70 (the agreed, fixed price), locking in a $5 gain. The $5 loss on the first deal and the $5 gain on the second deal cancel each other out. The trader was long one cargo and short another cargo; she combined a long and short position to make her overall position flat. She was hedged.

What if the market had risen (prices had gone up)? We know that the long position is happy when prices go up (we checked the formulas and found the right Smiley face). What about the other position? It is a short position and we expect rising prices to give us a Frowny Face.

This time the market goes up to $80 a barrel and stays there for two months. The long position in tank looks great since it is sold at $80 (Platts average for the month) to the first buyer and makes a $10 per barrel profit. The Smiley Face has a grin a million dollars wide! The short sale doesn't look so good. The trader has to cover the position by buying oil at $80 a barrel (the market price) and sell it at the agreed fixed price of $70 to his other buyer. She makes a $10 loss, a $1 million dollar hit. The $10 profit and the $10 loss cancel each other out.

This unfortunate situation, where the hedge wipes out the windfall gain on the original position, is a basic feature of hedging. In order to cancel out the Frown, you have to accept that the Smile is canceled as well. A perfect hedge makes you flat. You no longer care which way the market moves. The price of avoiding massive losses from unpredictable market movements is that you have to give up the wild profits you might make.

While we are talking about massive losses and wild profits, let's revisit our fuel trader with his 50,000 mt and his decision to either lock in the price or take a chance on floating prices. When he realized he was long at the end of the week, he had to choose whether to sell right away at $391 and lock in his $20 per mt loss or wait and hope the market went up. We saw that the potential to lose money was so great that it could risk his job, possibly his career, if he just closed his eyes and prayed for higher prices. It made sense from all points of view to sell the cargo immediately at $391, take the loss and move on, hopefully to better trades.

When I ask students if they would hedge a position and explain that hedging means locking in the result at whatever the market price is, their answers often depend on the P&L of the position. This is perfectly normal and perfectly dangerous. Humans, which all traders are despite appearances in some cases, are irrational. We hate losses much more than we like gains, so we will do almost anything to avoid admitting to or taking losses. If we have a losing position, e.g., we bought at $100 and the market is now at $90, we often don't believe it's a real loss until we close the position or lock in a sale price. As long as we hold on, there is a chance the market might rise. The farther it falls, the more we are convinced that it now has to rise again. This goes on until we are dragged out of the office by security and tossed onto the sidewalk. So the students will say they would hedge a position that is making money; sometimes they say it needs to make more first, then they will hedge. However, students very often (more than fifty percent of the time) say they would not hedge a position that is losing money. While they are mostly happy to lock in a profit, they refuse to lock in a loss. This is called Loss Avoidance and is a powerful bias or human flaw.

The students I teach are little different from most of the traders I have known over the years. All of them think alike. The difference between the students and good traders is that good traders know they have to overcome this human weakness and hedge anyway, or the traders are forced to hedge by their company. Not all traders comply or behave rationally, and sometimes traders run up large losses because they think a loss is not real until it is locked in by a sale or a hedge. Though some might not like to admit it, I am sure that all traders have faced this problem at least once in their careers. If this subject (the psychology of trading) interests you, please look into various books and articles on behavioral finance by such great minds as Kahneman and Thaler.[2]

6.3   Imperfect Hedging or Basis Risk

So a hedge can be done by using offsetting physical contracts that use the same market prices. The problem with hedging with physical cargoes is that it is rarely easy to align the risks so they offset just the right way. A hedge needs to be opposite in direction: if we are long, we need to sell something at a fixed price (create a short position). It needs to be equal in size: if we are long 50,000 mt, we need to sell 50,000 mt. The market price should be the same: if we are long Platts Dated Brent prices, we should sell something whose market value is measured by Platts Dated Brent prices. The timing needs to be the same: if we are long a cargo that we will sell using the monthly average of Platts Dated Brent prices during July, we should sell a hedge whose value will be related to the prices of Platts Dated Brent during the month of July. When we hedge, we want to protect the price of our oil. Anything in our hedge that is different from the prices being used to sell the physical oil we are protecting will mean that our hedge is not perfect.

Can we use physical positions that rely on different market prices? The short answer is yes, but the long answer is that while this can be done, it doesn't offset all the risk and may even increase losses. Imagine that instead of selling 100,000 bbl of crude oil to hedge our in-tank position, we sold 150,000 bbl of jet fuel at a fixed price. We have two problems. First, the price of jet fuel and the price of crude oil don't always go up and down together. Sometimes, like during wars, the price of jet goes up much faster than crude

---

[2] I recommend Thinking Fast and Slow by Daniel Kahneman as well as Misbehaving: The Making of Behavioral Economics by Richard Thaler. Both are accessible introductions to a fascinating field that cuts across psychology, philosophy, economics, and finance.

oil. Sometimes, like during the COVID pandemic, the price of jet fuel goes down much faster than crude oil prices. We have a difference in the size of the cargo of crude oil and the size of the jet cargo; we sold 50,000 bbl more of jet than we have of crude. Let's see what these differences might do to us.

Suppose that instead of selling a cargo of crude at $70, we sold the jet fuel at $75 per barrel. We tried to sell only 100,000 bbl but the only buyer of jet fuel at a fixed price would only buy if the quantity were 150,000. Let's assume that there is a small war somewhere, just alarming enough to make the oil markets nervous even if it does not directly involve anyone in the Middle East. Immediately, oil prices shoot up. Since modern warfare uses lots of jet fuel and the supply of jet is typically very inelastic (it's hard to make a lot more when you need it), the price goes up faster than crude oil. Crude oil rises to $75 a barrel but jet fuel rises to $90 a barrel. The market stays like this until the war fizzles out or the UN steps in a month or two later. What happened to the trader?

His physical cargo of oil in tank did well again. He made a $5 a barrel profit. Since he has studied his Smiley Faces and his Frowny Faces, he knows that his hedge has probably canceled out this windfall gain. When he checks his jet fuel position he is dismayed to find that he has to buy jet fuel in the market at $90. He is losing $15 a barrel on his jet trade. On top of that, the quantities don't match. The trader is making $500,000 on the crude oil (100,000 bbl × $5/bbl profit) but he is losing $2,225,000 on the jet fuel (150,000 bbl × $15/bbl). The "hedge" has cost him $1.75 million because while he did the opposite trade (he sold something when he was long), he sold a different thing in a different size.

These differences between the hedge and the underlying deal that is being hedged are called "basis risks." Anytime a hedge is imperfect, it creates a basis risk. So hedging crude oil using jet fuel prices creates a basis risk which is the difference in movement between jet fuel and crude oil prices. Hedging a position with a different size hedge creates a basis risk. Basis risk can also be created by hedging different markets (e.g., by using WTI crude oil prices in the US instead of Brent when the cargo is priced using Dated Brent), different timing, or even different currencies ("quanto" hedges such as selling crude swaps in Pound Sterling to hedge a Platts price which is in USD).

In the case of our jet fuel hedge, we saw that the trader was unable to find a physical cargo hedge for less than 150,000 bbl; once he chose to sell a fixed price jet fuel cargo, this basis risk was imposed on him. It could have been the same for crude oil; he might not have found a buyer for 100,000 bbl of crude oil either. Sometimes traders decide that they don't want to hedge the exact amount of their position. They decide intentionally to under-hedge or over-hedge. An old boss of mine called this "optimizing the hedge." Even back then, in my first year of trading, I called it "speculating or gambling." What does it mean when you are long 100,000 and decide to optimize the hedge by only selling 50,000 bbl when you could sell 100,000? It simply means you are now long 50,000 bbl. What about selling 150,000 bbl when you could sell just 100,000? It means you are now short 50,000 bbl. Pretending that a long or short position are parts of a hedge is a sneaky way to justify to the rational part of our brains and to our managers that we are certainly not gambling, but merely "optimizing our hedges."

If you are interested in working out more examples of price risk and hedging after you have read this book, you can try the exercises in the accompanying hedging and risk workbook (available as a download on the book's page on Chapter 6). The exercises run from simple to complex including floating price deals and contango hedging; complete answers with in-depth explanations are provided in the answer book.

7

Using Basis Risk as a Trading Strategy

7.1 Examples of Basis Risk Hedging: Crude Oil Pricing

Early on in this book, I said that a trader's first job is to create risk. If, by managing his risk, he eliminates it completely (we saw that this is impossible in practice but he can get pretty close), it means he also eliminates any further chance of making money. A perfect hedge locks the result in. Most traders are not permitted to buy ten million barrels of oil, wait a few months, and, if they were right, close the position and spend the rest of the year playing computer games while they wait for their bonus. The days of huge, speculative positions are gone, and traders like Vitol, Mercuria, and Glencore claim to hedge all their positions. So how do they make money then, other than by having better operators, a more qualified shipping department, and better access to capital? The answer is that they use basis risk in their favor.

If a trader is long one million barrels of West African crude oil (Platts Dated Brent pricing[1]), his company will require him to hedge it. They won't generally say how he is to hedge it, though. The trader could use this cargo to express a view he has on the relationship between Dated Brent and Dubai. He believes that Dubai will weaken versus Brent. If Brent drops, he believes Dubai will drop more. If Brent goes up, he believes Dubai will go up less. So, to hedge his Dated Brent cargo (it is West African crude oil, but its value is

---

[1] African crude oil is priced using floating price formulas based on Platts Dated Brent. This is true for both term and spot contracts FOB West Africa, FOB North Africa and delivered into Asia (e.g., CIF China).

based on Brent prices so from a risk point of view, it is a Platts Dated Brent cargo), he sells one million barrels of Dubai at a fixed price.

Let's assume the West African cargo is worth Platts Dated Brent plus $2/bbl. Let's say the Dated Brent is $70/bbl. The trader sells a cargo of Dubai at $68/bbl (which is Dated Brent minus $2). He is now long Platts Dated Brent prices and short Platts Dubai prices. If we check our Smiley Faces and Frowny Faces, his hedge has created a spread position. He is no longer indifferent to how the prices move (recall that in our early hedges, the traders did not care if the prices went up or down; this only started to matter when the trader used jet fuel to hedge crude oil), since the two prices are different. The trader would still like Dated Brent prices to go up since his cargo will be valued (sold) based on those prices, but he would like Dubai prices to go down at the same time since his hedge is based on Dubai prices.[2] A "perfect" hedge would use Dated Brent prices to hedge a cargo that will be sold using Dated Brent pricing. So if the price of the Dated Brent valued cargo went down, the price of the Dated Brent valued derivative would also go down and vice versa. Instead the trader hedges Dated Brent prices by using Dubai prices as his hedge.

The trader turns out to be right about the market. The heavy sour crude oil market in Asia weakens while there is new turmoil in Libya, making light, sweet crudes more valuable in Europe. When the trader sells his cargo he sees that Dated Brent is now at $74/bbl and he sells his cargo at Dated Brent + $2, making a $4/bbl profit. He must also buy back his Dubai hedge (which he sold for $68). He discovers that Dubai has weakened despite the rise in Brent prices and he can buy back his cargo for $67, earning him a profit of $1/bbl. Overall, he makes $5/bbl.[3] This is only possible because his hedge is not the same thing as his underlying cargo. If this could work one way, isn't there a risk that something similar to the crude oil hedged with jet fuel could happen? Suppose Brent had gone down but Dubai had gone up. Then the hedge would not have worked and the trader would have lost money on both positions.

Traders understand this and so does their management. Basis risk is one of the tools traders use to create risk, but it's a risk that is generally far less dangerous than not hedging at all. If the trader accepts that there is a basis risk between Brent and Dubai, he might assess it as being worth $2/bbl. That

---

[2] Because the two prices, Brent and Dubai, are different, they can move in opposite directions. They might move in the same direction, up or down, but one moves faster than the other.

[3] I did not show tables and calculations for this exercise so I recommend that you work it out yourself on sheet of paper or on a spreadsheet. If you get a different answer than me, send me an email!

means he thinks that if Brent prices drop (he loses money on his long position), Dubai prices might not drop as far but the spread between them won't widen by more than $2/bbl. This makes a lot of sense. If we hedge Brent prices with WTI prices and Brent drops by $30/bbl, it is almost certain that WTI has also fallen by something close to $30/bbl. Even if WTI has fallen by only $27/bbl, this would mean a $3 million loss on our one million barrel cargo. But without a hedge, we would have lost $30 million. So management is willing to accept a certain amount of basis risk since they know the traders have created this risk based on their expert views of the market. No traders know exactly where crude oil prices are going, but many traders can confidently predict how certain prices, like Brent and Dubai, will move in relation to each other.

This use of basis risk to create opportunities is perhaps a "perversion" of hedging but it is a common thing. For now, we will try to restrict ourselves to the best possible hedging or "perfect" hedging. If a basis risk exists, we will address that and see if there is a better way to hedge. It would be more accurate to say that using basis risk to create positions is "spread trading." Traders commonly create these types of positions as they seek to profit from their understanding of the market without going outright long or short.

Using physical cargoes to hedge physical positions is possible but often unwieldy and complicated. The trader needs to find a cargo of the same size with the same price basis (same market price and same timing). The cargo has to be financed, loaded, and discharged. There are inspectors and brokers to pay. And something will always go wrong, whether it is the vessel sinking or just a one-day delay. It is also likely to be very difficult to find a seller or a buyer for a full cargo of oil at a fixed price. Using physical to hedge positions is not a great idea. Instead we need something that protects us against the price moving adversely but which doesn't involve physical cargoes.

7.2 Basis Risk and Hedging: Shipping Diesel from Asia to Europe

Suppose we are selling a cargo of diesel in Europe and the price will be calculated based on the average of the Platts price for the month of August. Our cargo will be loading in Asia and the FOB purchase price will be fixed within a day or two of sailing since it is based on three days around the B/L date. If we blindly sail to Europe, we may be shocked to discover that diesel prices have collapsed by the time we get there. So, to offset the risk, we call up a friend who works at an investment bank. He is a big-time trader who loves to gamble. We know that to offset the losses that happen when the market drops, we need to do something that makes money when prices drop. So we make a bet with our friend. We both agree that the European market for diesel is $600/mt. We bet him the price will be lower than that in August. How big a bet should we make? The bet should be as big as our cargo. So if our cargo is 60,000 mt, then we bet him 60,000 mt worth.

Our vessel sails to Europe and discharges. We watch in dismay as the market prices drop steadily all through August. On 1 August, the Platts price for diesel was still $600, but by the 15th it has dropped to $580. By the end of the month, European diesel is at $560 and the monthly average Platts price is $582. Our cargo of 60,000 just lost $1,080,000. Ouch. We call up our friend at the investment bank to moan about our loss and settle our bet. The trader tells us we won the bet and he will be sending us a check to cover his losses. What size check will we get? Well, we bet him that the Platts monthly average would be below $600 and it was! Platts was $582 for the month of August. We made $18/mt on our bet. Since the size of our bet was 60,000 mt, the check is for $1,080,000. The loss on the cargo is perfectly offset by the gain on our bet. What if the market had gone up instead? How would our physical deal and the bet worked out?

In this case, the physical cargo would be sold for, say, $625/mt, giving us a $25/mt profit on the cargo (a hefty $1.5 million if you have not done the math yourself). Unfortunately, when we call our friend to gloat about our trading skills and ask him what color Maserati we should buy, he asks us when we will be sending him his check for $1.5 million. We lost the bet we made with him! We bet the market would be lower than $600 and were wrong by $25. We owe him $25/mt on 60,000 mt or $1.5 million dollars. The hedge has once again offset the physical cargo…which is exactly what it is supposed to do. In both cases, the bet with our friend was about only one thing, the price of diesel. Since hedging is about protecting ourselves against adverse price movements, this is a pretty good hedge.

Before we move on to real derivatives like futures and swaps, I would like to look at this last hedge one more time. We could use the other examples, but since this hedge is purely about price, it's a good one to use. I have not bothered to mention anything about the cost of the oil or how we paid for it in Asia (Platts, Argus, EFP, etc.). I did not mention it because it really doesn't matter for hedging purposes. Once the cargo is sold into Europe using Platts European Diesel (there is no such quote, by the way. There are Platts Diesel prices for that market but they are called by other names.), we are worried about that price and that price alone. The price we paid for the cargo is already fixed in this scenario; it is too late to change it. So if we paid $1000/

7 Using Basis Risk as a Trading Strategy

mt or $25/mt in Asia, our hedging decisions will be the same. The market doesn't care if we are making or losing money, and even if we do, there is nothing we can do about it now. We must hedge the cargo, and when we do, we lock in the P&L (profit and loss) whether it is a gain or a loss. Of course, we do need to calculate our P&L if only to know if we should bother coming back to the office tomorrow. So let's assume that our cargo was bought at $550/mt and there is $30/mt in freight, inspection, interest, and other costs to ship the oil to Europe. So the cargo lands into Europe at $580.

Let's look at a few possibilities.

In the first case, we make the bet with our friend at the same level as before, $600 for the month of August. We bet the price will be lower than that level.

If the Platts average price for August is $620, we sell the cargo at that price and make $40/mt. We then pay our friend $20/mt to settle the bet. We made $40 on the cargo and lost $20 on the hedge for a net profit of $20/mt. So it is just as if we sold the cargo at a fixed price of $600/mt.

If the Platts average price is $570, we sell the cargo at that price and lose $10/mt. We then get paid $30/mt when we settle our bet with the banker. We lost $10 on the cargo and made $30 on the hedge for a net profit of $20/mt. So it is just as if we sold the cargo at $600/mt.

If you can see where this is going, then you understand what it means to hedge. Try working out different results with the same level of bet ($600) but with the market price moving to whatever number you want. Try $1/mt. Try $10,000/mt. The result is always the same. The final P&L is determined by where you set the level of the bet. Let's look at a different case where the bet is made at a different level of price.

This time our gambling trader friend will only take the bet if we agree to a lower starting point since the market is weaker and he is a bit hungover and unwilling to take too much risk today. Instead of $600, we agree that the starting point for the bet will be $590/mt. Again, we bet the market will be lower; this will compensate us if our cargo loses value. For some of you, it will be obvious what this does to our final P&L. For many of you, since this is probably all new, we need to work it out first (something I needed to do for quite a while when I first started hedging cargoes).

The bet is set at $590. If the Platts monthly average is lower, the trader pays us. If Platts is higher, we pay the trader. The same physical deal applies as before; we are selling the cargo on the Platts monthly average.

If the market goes up to $650, we make $70/mt on our physical cargo (recall that the cargo's delivered cost is $580). We then settle our bet, which we lost, and pay our friend $60/mt (the difference between our bet of $590 and the market level of $650). In the end we made $70 on the cargo and lost

$60 on the bet, so we made a total of $10/mt. It is as if we sold the cargo at a fixed price of $590.

If the market drops to $500, our physical cargo loses $80/mt. Our bet pays off, though, and we receive $90 from the trader. Our net profit is $10/mt. It is as if we sold the cargo at a fixed price of $590.

7.3 A Quick Summary of Risk and Hedging

Before we conclude the theoretical discussions on hedging and move on to the instruments (derivatives), take a moment to ask yourself about the bet and position it created. Since we used it as a hedge, it made us flat. What about our trader friend? If he did not have any other positions before making that bet, what was his position once he made it? And what if we made that bet without any physical or other long position? What would our position be? If you use the Long and Short formulas and the Smiley and Frowny Faces, you can easily find the answers. If not, keep reading.

As you can see from all these examples, the P&L of the deal, when the price risk is perfectly hedged, depends on the price at which the hedge is executed. In this case, we talked about a bet, but this bet is a derivative. After all, a derivative is nothing more than a financial deal (no physical delivery) in which the settlement price depends on the market price. In this case, the bet was set at a fixed price (the price from which we measured if the market went up or down), and the winner would be determined by calculating the average price of physical diesel cargoes in the market; the settlement price of the bet is "derived" from the underlying physical market.

Once the position is hedged, the P&L is locked in. If the hedged sales price is below the cost (buying price) of the cargo, then the hedge locks in a loss. This is one of the reasons many of my students don't want to hedge a losing position; they realize that once it is hedged, the loss is permanent. Please don't follow that logic. Always remember that things could get a lot worse and cost you your job and your mental health. Recall the sage advice of the world's top oil traders: Great traders know how to cut their losses. That means accept the loss, hedge it, and move on to better deals.

All of these cases and examples demonstrate the fundamentals of hedging. It is all about neutralizing the Frowny Face. The Smiley Face also gets neutralized when we hedge but that is the price we pay for avoiding catastrophic losses. The hedge is opposite in direction: if we are long, we need to sell something at a fixed price. The hedge is equal in size; if we are short 400,000 bbl, we need to buy 400,000 bbl of hedge. The hedge covers the same prices we are worried about, not the prices that are already past or which concern different places and times; if we are selling our cargo based on September average jet fuel in Singapore, we need to hedge that specific price. To recap:

A hedge is: Opposite in direction
              The same size
              The same market price
              The same period of time

If any of these conditions are not met, the hedge is imperfect and creates basis risk.[4]

---

[4] Sometimes perfect hedges can't found or the trader wants the basis risk. It takes statistical analysis and good data to say whether or not a very bad hedge is better or worse than no hedge. For example, if you are long one million barrels of crude oil and the only thing you can find to hedge are Tokyo red bean futures priced in yen, is your position better or worse with the hedge? The answer is not obvious though I would instinctively say such a hedge would be pointless at best.

8

Basic Derivatives

We have already defined derivatives, and those of you who want more formal, financial definitions can find them readily in any finance textbook or on the internet. For now, we will simply say that they are financial contracts whose settlement price is based on the price of an underlying physical market. The bets we made with our trader friend are derivatives; the bet was for 60,000 mt of Platts European diesel, but the bet was settled by paying in dollars, not by delivering physical oil. We only cared about the price, and the price of the bet was derived (taken from, calculated based on, etc.) from the price of physical cargoes of diesel published by Platts. We don't generally call these "bets" since traders don't like to be called gamblers, and shareholders don't like the idea of some overpaid 25-year-old gambling with their money. We call these kinds of bets "derivatives and hedges."

Since we started our discussion of hedging with these "bets," I will continue with them and introduce our first derivative, the swap. The swap was not the first derivative to be used in oil trading; indeed, the first oil swap based on Platts prices was done in NY only in 1985. Despite their recent innovations in oil (currency and interest rate swaps have traded for far longer), they have become widespread and liquid across most oil markets.

8.1 Swaps

When I teach oil trading and risk management, I usually start with futures because they are generally considered the simplest derivatives to explain and are already familiar to most people in and out of the market. People outside the industry know about WTI futures and the price of crude oil even if they don't really know what futures are. This time, though, since we are fresh from using bets to explain hedging, I will start with swaps.

The "bet" we used to hedge our cargo is nothing more or less than a swap. If you recall the barbaric definition I quoted on the first page, you will know that a swap is a financial instrument based on the exchange of a fixed income stream against a floating income stream. With a bit of thought and analysis, we can now understand this in the context of our positions and the bets we made. The bets involved a fixed price so that is what "fixed income stream" must mean; we "sold" 60,000 mt of diesel at $600/mt.[1] The initial bet is more of a one-shot deal than a stream, but that is just mere vocabulary. The "stream" comes from the idea that our swap (our bet) covers a series of prices, in our case the prices over the course of a month for calculating who won the bet. That is our stream of purchases at a fixed price. The settlement of our bet was determined by the floating prices in the market (Platts). We had to buy back our 60,000 mt, pricing in a bit every day at the numbers published by Platts.

So a swap has a fixed price side and a floating price side, just like our bet. If you have worked out the Long and Short formulas for the bets we made (I will start calling them swaps now), you know that we went short the swap and our friend went long. We therefore sold the swap and he bought it. Of course, we also had to buy back the floating price (and the trader sold the floating price) as the swap was settled, but the industry convention is that the fixed price determines who is the buyer and who is the seller. If you buy a swap, you are long. If you sell a swap, you are short. We sold a swap at $600 for August average Platts European diesel prices. (Since this was a hedge, we ended up flat, but if there had been no physical position, we would have been short 60,000 mt.)

Before we move on, let's look at another example of a swap. This time let's look at buying a swap. Based on what we discussed, you already know that buying a swap is the same as betting that the market will rise. So a buyer of a swap is getting long. We need to know what the price of the swap is and how we will measure the market to see if it went up or down. So the swap deal must include a fixed price, a method for measuring the price, a price reference, and a time period. Let's say you are buying an October Singapore Kerosene (MOPS kero or Mean of Platts Singapore Kerosene cargoes) swap for $87 per barrel.

---

[1] Check the Frowny Faces. If we made the bet that the market would be lower than $600, we are unhappy if it goes up. That means we are short, so it's like selling 60kt of diesel at $600.

Swap: 50,000 bbl of October MOPS kero

Bought at $87 per bbl

Position: long 50,000 bbl

Settlement: based on the monthly average of the Platts Mean quotations for Kerosene FOB Singapore during the month of October.

Platts reports market prices for kerosene in Singapore on every working day. These are the floating prices or "floating income stream." On each day, one of the monthly prices is set, turned from a floating price into a fixed price. At the end of the month you take the average of all these prices and see if it higher or lower than $87 per bbl. Since you are long, you would like the price to be higher (we bought the swap at $87 and would like to sell or settle it at a higher price.).

Platts October Kero Monthly Average Price: $90 per bbl

You bought the swap at a fixed price of $87 and sell it back at $90 for a profit of $3 per bbl. You earn $150,000 on the swap.

Swaps are used because they are simple and can be created for any market we choose. The caveat is that the buyer and the seller need to agree on how to measure the market or calculate the prices. For this reason, swaps are transacted based on reliable, relevant, public prices such as those we find in Platts, Argus, or the futures exchanges. This means that we determine the market level (the floating side of the swap) by using reputable sources that we trust to provide accurate and representative market prices.

Since swaps are designed to hedge price risk on physical cargoes, it makes sense to trade swaps that use the same prices as the physical deals. Again, this means prices from Platts, Argus, and futures exchanges. It is theoretically possible to enter into a swap agreement for anything you want, but if it doesn't relate to your price risk, you are creating basis risk and possibly opening yourself up to being cheated.

Imagine you enter into a swap with Caltex for 500,000 bbl of jet fuel based on the Caltex Bahrain Posted Price. The Caltex Bahrain Posted Price is set entirely by Caltex and is no longer used by the market, though it still might be used for very small, local parcels around Bahrain (small barges or truck loads). Let's assume you buy the swap because you think the Caltex price is too low versus the international jet market and Platts prices. So you are long the Caltex price and now obviously hope and expect Caltex to raise their posted prices; if they do, you will make money on your swap. Unfortunately for you, Caltex hardly sells anything using their posted price so even if they lowered it to zero, it would not cost them much on physical sales. Their only risk position is the swap they traded with you. Since they are short the swap, they can lower their posted price as far as they like and earn millions on the swap.

Now, the Caltex Posted Price has been published for decades and was often used in sales contracts throughout the region. The Caltex Bahrain Posted Price was used for several contracts in East Africa and the Indian Ocean. Even back then the price was disconnected from the market and always higher than Platts and other more reliable reference prices. We would buy our oil using Platts and resell it using the higher Caltex prices. The price is set entirely by someone working at Caltex Bahrain, and though the prices are generally somewhere around the market, they can be anywhere from a few cents to a few dollars per barrel different, usually higher. Obviously, trading a swap against Caltex when they can set their own settlement prices (the "floating income stream" of the swap) is likely to be an unhappy experience. Ask yourself this, if we made a heads or tails bet for $1 million dollars and I flipped the coin without you there, would you take my word for it that you lost? I hope not. And for the same reason, we don't trade swaps based on Caltex Posted Prices or other unreliable prices (prices that don't necessarily reflect the market or prices whose calculations we can't explain or understand).

There are even some Platts prices which are not reliable enough for some companies to accept as the underlying price for swaps. When I worked for an investment bank in Singapore, I wanted to trade swaps based on Mean of Platts Arab Gulf (MOPAG) prices for gasoil, jet, and fuel oil. This was an illiquid swaps market to begin with very few deals done in that market, and those deals were generally of small size. The middle office did not understand how Platts calculated the MOPAG prices and was not comfortable with the basis risk those swaps would have created. Effectively, if I went long a MOPAG swap, I could not hope to sell it back into the market or hedge the position directly. The only way to manage MOPAG risk is by trading Mean of Platts Singapore (MOPS) swaps. My management was not happy with the relationship between the two, though I suspect it had more to do with them lacking the competence to enter a new derivative into the computer system since the correlation between MOPS and MOPAG was exceedingly high and could be hedged with other swaps (freight swaps to be precise).[2]

---

[2] Platts Arab Gulf prices are calculated by subtracting shipping costs from Singapore prices. This is historical since products used to flow from the AG to the East. Additionally, there were almost

Most swaps therefore trade based on the most liquid, transparent, and relevant markets. Most of the time these markets refer to prices published by Platts, but we can trade swaps whose settlement price is based on the official prices published by futures exchanges as well since those are highly liquid, transparent, relevant, reliable, and understandable prices. For these reasons, the main swaps markets involve such prices as MOPS Diesel, MOPS Kero, Platts Rotterdam barges for various products, Platts Dated Brent, WTI, and Platts US Gulf Coast cargoes for products like gasoline and diesel. That is not an exhaustive list, of course, and it is also possible to find swaps for what could be considered low liquidity and poorly transparent markets like the Mediterranean (Platts Med prices).

When a published price is not reliable, transparent, or liquid, it is often simply not used by physical traders. For example, traders in the Middle Eastern market prefer to use Platts Dubai swaps instead of Oman futures to hedge their cargoes despite sometimes severe basis risk because the Dubai swaps market is familiar and highly liquid. Traders in North West Europe and West Africa commonly buy and sell distillates using ICE gasoil prices rather than Platts cargo prices because ICE gasoil is highly liquid, transparent, and flexible (as a hedging tool). This means that when traders are looking to hedge their risk, they don't necessarily look for a swap based on where they are selling their cargo (e.g., into the Med), but instead they look for a swap which is based on the price they are using to buy or sell the physical oil. Many Platts prices are infrequently used by physical traders and almost never used by swaps traders for these reasons.

We have said that our bet with our friend at the bank was a swap, and it is. In that example, we sold 60,000 mt of Platts European Diesel at $600/mt. The settlement of the swap (determining who won the bet) was based on the average of the prices published by Platts for European Diesel during the calendar month of August. This is a very typical kind of swap, except perhaps for the size which is fairly big. Most swaps tend to trade in traditional sizes whose origin is unknown (to me at least). European product swaps are typically for 5000 mt and are based on a monthly average. Singapore swaps are usually 50,000 bbl. US swaps are also 50,000 bbl. The exceptions to this are fuel oil swaps. Fuel oil is priced in USD/MT all around the world so the swap size is traditionally 5000 mt. It is possible to trade almost any size swap from small quantities like 387 mt up to 250,000 mt (or 2 million barrels) per month, though most trades are for 5000–25,000 mt (or 50,000–250,000 bbl).

---

never any fixed price trades in the AG market while Singapore had fixed priced trades, swaps, and occasionally a futures market for products.

Swaps can be bought and sold for almost any period. We refer to this as the tenor of the swap. If a swap is settled using all the prices published by Platts during the month of June, we say it is a full month June swap, a calendar June swap, or just a June swap. If the swap is settled using the prices from the beginning of January through the end of December, we call this a calendar swap. If we buy a 5000 mt June swap, we are long 5000 mt. If we buy a 5000 mt calendar swap, we are long 60,000 mt (5000 mt per month × 12 months). It is possible to buy multi-year swaps, half-year swaps, and quarterly swaps; the position (long or short) is determined by multiplying the number of months by the nominal size of the swap. So if you buy 10kt of Q1 swap, you are long 30,000 mt. Bear this in mind if you need to hedge 24,000 mt over the entire year. If you sell a calendar swap for 24,000 mt, you will find yourself short 288,000 mt. You should instead sell a 2000 mt calendar swap. If you are new to this, don't hesitate to clearly explain to your broker or your counterparty exactly what you want and are trying to achieve.

If you trade a one-month swap, the settlement is made shortly (a few working days) after the end of the month. If you trade a calendar swap, each month is settled individually. So if you buy a 50,000 bbl calendar 2023 MOPS diesel swap for $79/bbl, you will make or receive payment twelve times. If the Platts average for January is $80, you get paid $50,000 ($1/bbl × 50,000 bbl). If February Platts average is $78, you pay out $50,000 (−$1/bbl × 50,000 bbl). And so on for the rest of the year.

While 50,000 bbl and 5000 mt full month swaps are traditional and the most liquid swaps, it is possible to trade nearly anything these days. Investment banks and the derivative desks of oil majors and traders will buy and sell swaps for "odd" sizes like 1750 mt and "odd" periods like the 13th to the 23rd of the month. In liquid markets, these "odd" swaps accumulate in a trader's book and either cancel each other out or build up into a standard monthly swap. If a trader sells 2500 mt of swap for the first week to one client, then 2500 mt for the second week to another, and so on, he ends up short 10,000 mt of monthly swap (recall our discussion on getting long and short; buying over a five day average is the same as buying equal fifths of oil each priced on one of the five days). The swaps work the same way, of course, since they are designed to hedge physical pricing. These partial swaps ("odd" lots) settle at the end of their pricing periods. So if you buy a swap for 1–5 July, the settlement will be made a few working days after the 5th and not at the end of the month.

8.2 Cleared Swaps, Futures Exchanges, and Counterparty Risk

Swaps are usually over-the-counter (OTC) financial instruments. We can enter into swap deals with anyone we want and use any prices or references we like. They are mostly unregulated. If you trade stocks or futures contracts, you are required to comply with certain laws, rules, and regulations. The shares and futures are clearly defined and standardized. About the only things that regulate swaps are banking rules governing risk and collateral and the company's own policies on risk. Swaps are by definition instruments which create a position. If a company enters into a swap, it runs the risk of not getting paid if the counterparty goes bankrupt or simply vanishes. This risk is very low on controlled exchanges where the counterparty is the exchange itself. For this reason, most trading companies and banks are required to hold assets to offset some of the risk involved in trading swaps in unregulated, OTC markets.

Since the Financial Crisis and the introduction of Basel II banking rules, most companies have become very wary of financial risk. During the worst of the crisis, companies like Glencore and even Goldman Sachs were rumored to be going bankrupt; their credit was no good and they could not trade OTC swaps in the market. Basel II banking rules meant that banks and trading companies needed to set aside large and onerous amounts of capital in case of defaults on their swaps positions. The market needed a solution that would restore both confidence and liquidity. This solution already existed but its application exploded starting in 2009.

If a company trades futures on an exchange, there is no capital requirement because the company is trading against a large, well-capitalized counterparty, the exchange clearing house. Additionally, the company must put up some collateral (give money as a security deposit) to the exchange to guaranty its performance. This meant that the company's risk was greatly reduced since the exchange itself (CME-Nymex or ICE) was very unlikely to disappear or go bankrupt abruptly. Any deals done with the exchange eliminated most counterparty risk. So if a company could trade a swap with the exchange instead of a dodgy trading company, it could avoid Basel II requirements and sleep peacefully at night.

The mechanism for achieving this is called a cleared swap. The idea is that the buyer and seller agree to a swap trade and also agree that it will be "cleared." The deal is concluded in the market either directly or through a broker. The broker then transfers the deal to the agreed exchange where both parties have trading accounts. The deal is basically broken into two deals with the exchange replacing the counterparty for both traders. So if I buy a swap from Mercuria and we agree to clear it through ICE, my contract will be with the ICE clearing house; ICE will be selling the swap to me. Mercuria will end up selling the swap to ICE. The contractual relationship between me and Mercuria stops when the swap is cleared except for our obligations to the broker for commissions. I no longer have to worry about Mercuria's credit or my own banking regulation collateral. My OTC swap has been turned into an exchange-traded "futures" contract. The vast majority of swaps traded on the market are cleared on one of the exchanges. This means that the swaps must be standardized to a large degree and in a contract form that is acceptable to the exchange. The exchanges publish a list of swaps which they accept to clear.[3]

8.3   Some Problems with Swaps

The examples we have used so far seem to show that swaps are a perfect hedge. While a standard swap covers the entire monthly average while physical cargoes are typically priced using only three or five days of prices, it is possible to enter into a swap for specific dates. So if a vessel is going to have a bill of lading on the 13th and the physical pricing is based on three quotations (prices) published by Platts around the B/L date, we could buy or sell a swap based on the average of 11, 12, and 13 of the month. Unfortunately, this is still not perfect.

We already discussed how there can be operational delays with any physical delivery. The delay could range from few minutes to many months. If the contract is linked to the COD date and the vessel is stuck in the load port for a month, it is clear that any hedge that was put in place based on an estimated arrival date with discharge a few days later will no longer apply. If the vessel is sold on the basis of the average of the weekly Platts prices for the week of arrival and we estimate the vessel will arrive on the 29th of the month, we would hedge the last week of the month (e.g., 27–31) using a bespoke swap ("odd" timing). If the vessel arrives one month later our swap

---

[3] Almost all oil swaps between market participants (i.e., anyone who is not a client but is an active trader of derivatives) are cleared these days. Swaps looks the same but are called "futures" or, in the case of ICE, S2F which means Swaps To Futures. "Swaps" are also traded directly on ICE and the CME and are also legally futures contracts. This sleight of hand means that traders and oil companies don't become Financial Counterparties and subject to oversight and regulations under Dodd/Frank (USA) and EMIR (UK). This also means that traditional swaps brokers are losing business to the exchanges as well as falling under financial authority controls since they are now futures brokers. Old-fashioned swaps brokers now have to get certified and file seemingly endless compliance reports.

is already settled (it either made or lost money independently of the value of the cargo) and the price of our oil will float up and down for another month unless we put on another hedge. Even a one-day difference in the bill of lading date can have a significant impact on the hedging results if the market moves sharply from one day to the next. The problem is that swaps are fixed in price and in dates, while physical cargoes are subject to the whims of weather, port congestion, and anything else that delays loading, sailing, or discharge.

Swaps are traditionally traded in the sizes we discussed. If you buy a 50,000 bbl MOPS Kero swap, the settlement will be based on exactly 50,000 bbl. If you want to hedge a 300,000 bbl physical cargo, you will trade six swaps of 50,000 each (it is, of course, possible to trade larger sizes but 50k bbl is standard). If your contract is a typical Eastern FOB contract, it might have an operational tolerance of plus or minus ten percent; the FOB buyer can contractually load anywhere from 270,000 to 330,000 bbl. Assume you own the cargo on a fixed price, so you are long. Suppose you have sold this cargo to a trader at a floating price. You might decide to hedge your exposure by selling swaps. Since you don't know if the trader is going to lift the minimum or the maximum, you decide to hedge exactly 300,000 bbl (you sell 300,000 bbl of swaps). As the cargo is loading, your buyer decides to maximize the loading and take 330,000 bbl. The buyer might decide to do this whether the market is higher or lower; his decision depends on things like freight costs and his own contractual commitments to a third party.

Suppose you bought the cargo at $75 and you have hedged the cargo at $75/bbl with 300,000 bbl of swaps. The market drops to $65 and the trader decides to load 330k bbl. What happens to your P&L?

Physical cargo: Bought at $75 and sold at $65 = $10/bbl loss on 330k bbl or $3.3 million dollars

Hedge position: Sold at $75 and settles at $65 = $10/bbl gain on 300k bbl or $3.0 million dollars

Overall, the trade loses $300,000 despite being hedged because while you can control the hedge, you can't control the physical cargo within ten percent of either side of 300,000 bbl.

Is it possible to make adjustments as the cargo is loading? Possibly, though it is usually extremely hard to find a market for a swap that covers the following day or two days. In any case, any adjustments affect only the days that are left. So if this cargo was pricing over five days, the daily hedged volume was

60,000 bbl per day (5 days × 60,000 bbl = 300,000 bbl). The actual loaded quantity was 330,000 which works out to 66,000 bbl/day. You sell the physical buyer 66,000 bbl on the first, second, and third day while your hedge only covers 60,000 bbl per day. On the bill of lading date, it is definitely too late to adjust the swap for the first, second, and third (B/L) dates, so the position is automatically and irreversibly long 18,000 bbl. There is a very slim chance that you can adjust that position and correct the swaps for the remaining two days because the market rarely trades prompt, bespoke swaps, or will charge a hefty premium for doing so. You can still hedge but with something else such as futures or next month's swap.

These examples show how a swap can be used to hedge fixed price risk. Swaps can also be used to hedge risk when there is no fixed price. This might seem contradictory since I said that you get long by buying something at a fixed price and you get short by selling something at a fixed price. If you don't have a fixed price, how can you have a risk that should be hedged? One of the ways to have this kind of risk is by having a spread risk. We discussed spread risks when we first talked about basis risk.

Spread risk is the possibility of losing money because the buy contract and the sell contract use two different prices. For example, if you buy a cargo using Platts Dated Brent and resell the cargo using Platts Dubai price, you have a risk even if the contract is otherwise back-to-back on everything else including pricing dates (e.g., five around B/L). Platts Dated Brent and Platts Dubai are not the same price and don't represent the same market. Consequently, they can move in different ways. Remember that an ideal, perfect hedge is a derivative that is settled using the exact same price as is used to determine the price of the physical cargo.

Let's look at an example of risk we might encounter in a case like this:

8.4 Brent vs. Dubai Spread Risk: Another Look

A trader is loading a cargo of West African crude oil at the end of August. The one million barrel cargo is part of a term contract from a national oil company. The price is based on a five day average of Platts Dated Brent quotations plus a premium of $2/bbl. The five quotations are those immediately following the bill of lading date. The lifting is forty-five days away.

As it stands, there is no price risk since the cargo does not have any fixed prices yet and has not sold the cargo. There is certainly market risk since the trader would like to get a higher premium over Dated Brent. And there is always the remote possibility that the cargo cannot find a buyer at all and must be put into storage, or that is it delayed or canceled altogether. There is very little the trader can do about any of these possibilities; they are the kinds of risks the trader accepts as part of trading. Specifically, there are no markets for hedging premiums or discounts to Platts (e.g., the $2/bbl premium above Dated Brent).

The trader is approached by a Chinese oil company who is interested in buying the cargo FOB West Africa. They are willing to pay a good price, but they only want to buy using Platts Dubai prices. They agree to all the other terms and conditions of the trader's contract including the pricing days (five quotations following the B/L date). The Chinese buyer is keen so the trader thinks he can get a good price and earn a good profit on this cargo simply selling almost back-to-back. The trader looks at the market (he reads the latest edition of Platts) and calculates the following prices for the cargo based on Platts prices (Table 8.1):

According to the trader's calculation using the most recent Dated Brent and Dubai prices published by Platts, this deal will make the trader $1.5 million back-to-back. He doesn't need to find a vessel since he is selling FOB. The Chinese buyer is a first class international company with excellent credit. He is buying and selling on the same dates (same price quotations) so he doesn't worry about hedging. It looks like the perfect deal. The trader accepts the deal and starts planning how to decorate his new ski chalet in Verbier.

As the loading date approaches and the vessel arrives at the load port, the trader checks his P&L in the system. He is shocked to see that his $1.5 million profit is now a $500,000 loss. He calls the middle office to tell them there is a mistake and that they have obviously entered the wrong prices. The middle office explains that they are simply using the latest Platts prices for Dated Brent and Dubai. The trader rushes to read the most recent copies of Platts. He checks the latest prices and sees the following (Table 8.2):

When he rechecks his deal he sees that he is buying at $77/bbl (Dated Brent at $75 + $2 premium) and selling at $76.50 (Dubai at $70 +

Table 8.1 Analysis of prices for a sale of crude into Asia

Platts Oilgram Report for the day:		
	Dated Brent	$70
	Dubai	$67
Trader's contract:	Platts Dated Brent + $2/bbl	
	Platts Dated Brent	$70
	Premium	$2
	Contract price	$72/bbl
Chinese buyer's bid:	Platts Dubai + $6.50/bbl	
	Platts Dubai	$67
	Premium	$6.50
	Contract price	$73.50

Table 8.2 Prices for Dated Brent and Dubai for arbitrage trade

Platts Dated Brent:	$75
Platts Dubai:	$70

$6.50 premium). The North Sea market is undergoing maintenance, Libyan production has been reduced again and light sweet crude in the West has increased sharply. Meanwhile, Aramco has dropped its prices for this month and next as well as announced a production increase up to its full quota. Heavy sour crudes in the East have performed poorly even as the Brent benchmark has risen. The trader sadly realizes that his back-to-back trade was not locked in. Had he sold on a fixed price using the numbers on the day he did the deal, he would have been in big trouble, but he still lost $2 million dollars. (I say this because the original deal showed a profit of $1.5 million which turned into a $500k loss. This drop could have been prevented, so I would call this a loss! The loss is the difference between making $1.5 million and losing $500k.) What should the trader have done to prevent this loss of profit?

Let's check our Smiley Faces and Frowny Faces. We know there is a position because the trader's P&L changed. If you think about it simply and use the Face formula the other way around (start with prices for Brent and Dubai both going up and see what the conclusion is), we can tell that the trader would like Dated Brent prices to be low and Dubai prices to be high. If we use absurd prices to illustrate, we could say he would like free oil from his supplier which he sells to the Chinese buyer at $1 million per barrel. It's easier for me to think like this than to use real numbers from Platts. I don't even need to do the math to see that the trader is long one price and short the other. Which is which?

The trader would like free oil from his supplier which would imply Platts Dated Brent dropping to −$2/bbl (plus the premium of $2 would give an invoice price of zero). Bear in mind that this says nothing about Dubai prices, so let's assume Dubai prices don't move for now. If the trader wants Dated Brent lower, then he is short Dated Brent. If Dated Brent and Dubai prices always move in lock-step (perfect correlation of 1.00 for those who like math), then obviously if Dated drops by $70/bbl, so will Dubai. In the market, that is not the case, so the trader is short Dated Brent prices.

The trader would also like Dubai prices to go up to silly numbers (how high would it have to go so the trader gets a bonus that makes him the richest man in the world?). If rising Dubai prices make him happy, he must be long Dubai.

So the trader is short Dated Brent and long Dubai. He would like one to go up and one to go down. Or he would like one to go up and the other to go up less, and so on. He would like the spread (the difference in price) between the two prices to change. Specifically, he would like the Brent–Dubai spread to narrow. When he did the trade that spread was $3/bbl (Dated Brent over Dubai or Dated more expensive than Dubai by $3). He would have liked the spread to narrow to $1, for example. Instead, the spread widened to $5 which cost him $2 million. The trader did not have any outright price risk. He was not long one million barrels of oil. His overall price risk was hedged but his hedge had a basis risk. That basis risk is the difference in price between Platts Dated Brent and Platts Dubai. We would say the trader has an East–West or Brent–Dubai spread position. How could he have hedged this risk?

If the trader is short Dated Brent prices, he needs to buy a Dated Brent swap for his pricing days. Once he does so, he locks in his Dated Brent price. Let's say he buys a Dated Brent swap for $70. We know from our earlier exercises that no matter what happens to Dated Brent, the trader will pay $70 for his oil when the hedge is taken into account. He is now owns fixed price crude oil.

Some of you are scratching your heads because I said he was short Dated Brent, so if he buys a swap he should be flat! I sort of lied. The trader was short Dated Brent versus Dubai. His position is not really short Dated or long Dubai; he is long the spread between the two of them. This means that any hedge he makes should involve the spread, not just one of the prices. If the trader locks in the price of Dated Brent, he must also lock in the price of Dubai or he is just creating an outright price risk. Think of it this way, we know there is a risk if he does nothing (reread the scenario if that is unclear). If the trader hedges the purchase, he is turning his floating price purchase into a fixed price purchase. From there it is a classic example just like the ones we went through earlier. If the trader is long fixed price oil, he is worried the market will drop. In this scenario, he is worried that his sales price, Platts Dubai, will drop so he needs to hedge that price.

If the trader decides to hedge only his sales price by selling a Platts Dubai swap, he has now turned his floating price sale into a fixed price sale. He is now short. If the market price for Platts Dated Brent goes up, he will lose money. So he needs to now hedge his purchase by buying a Dated Brent swap.

So, at the same time the trader locks in his Dated Brent price by buying a Dated swap, he must lock in his Dubai price by selling a Dubai swap at $67. He has now locked in his purchase price ($70 + $2) and his sale price ($67 + $6.50). His P&L is now locked in at $1.5 million dollars. We can check this by rerunning his P&L including the swaps using the same prices that made him lose money (P + L of −$500k, see Table 8.3):

Feel free to set up a spreadsheet or do the calculations by hand using different settlement prices (the market Platts prices used to invoice the cargo and settle the swaps). Try widening the spread more, narrowing the spread, dropping prices by $25, or raising them by $100. Then do some exercises with different prices for the Dated Brent and Dubai swaps; move them apart or closer together and see what the results are. As always, you should find that the final P&L using the physical and the swaps should be determined by the fixed prices of the swaps you trade. Once the fixed prices of the swaps are set, the P + L for that particular scenario should not change no matter which way the market goes.

In a real trading situation, the trader would not buy a Dated Brent swap and then try to sell a Dubai swap. There is a liquid market for trading the two swaps at exactly the same time; this is called a spread trade. So the trader does

Table 8.3 P&L of crude oil arbitrage deal including hedging

Platts Dated Brent:	$75 (five days around B/L price)	
Platts Dubai:	$70 (five days around B/L price)	
Physical Cargo		
Purchase Price $77	(Dated + $2)	
Sale Price	$76.50	(Dubai + $6.50)
Loss	$500,000	(−$0.50/bbl)

Hedges
Dated Brent Swap for same calendar dates as the physical cargo pricing
The trader is buying the fixed price and selling back the floating Platts

Bought Dated Swap	$70 (fixed price leg of the swap)	
Platts Dated Prices	$75 (floating price leg of the swap)	
Profit	$5 million	($5/bbl)

Dubai Swap for same calendar dates as the physical cargo pricing
The trader is selling the fixed price and buying back the floating Platts

Sold Dubai Swap	$67 (fixed price leg of the swap)	
Platts Dubai Prices	$70 (floating price leg of the swap)	
Loss	$3 million	(−$2/bbl)

Net P&L
Physical Cargo	−$500,000
Dated Brent Swap	$5,000,000
Dubai Swap	−$3,000,000
Overall Result	$1,500,000

not even care what the price of Dated Brent swap is as long as he is locking in a Dated Brent price that is no worse $3 higher than the Dubai price. If the Brent swap is $400/bbl and the Dubai swap is $397, this is fine with the trader. The trader locks in the Brent–Dubai spread at $3. If the Dates Brent swap is $12 and the Dubai swap is $9, the result is still the same; a $3 spread is locked in. As an aside, when we are trading spreads like this, we call each side a "leg." We also call the two sides of a single swap "legs."

This hedge now works and gives the trader the result he was expecting. This kind of hedge will also work even if the pricing dates are different. Let's change the trade around. This time the Chinese buyer wants the crude oil delivered to Shanghai and wants a price linked to the delivery date. He is ready to pay Platts Dubai plus $8.50 for CIF Shanghai with pricing based on the average of the month of October (the higher premium covers the freight cost). Can the trader do this and still hedge the Brent–Dubai risk as he did before? The pricing dates are now different in addition to the Brent–Dubai spread. We can say the trader now has a "time spread" risk as well as a Brent–Dubai risk. Even if the Brent–Dubai relationship stays the same ($3 spread) all through the week of the cargo loads, the trader will be locking in a fixed price at the end of August once his cargo prices (five days after B/L) while he won't know his sale price until the end of October.

If the average of the five day Platts Dated Brent pricing in West Africa is $70, that implies that Dubai is $67 on average during those five days (we assume the spread stays at $3 between them). The trader pays $72 for his oil and calmly sails to Shanghai, confident in his view that the Brent–Dubai spread will stay at $3. At the end of October, he calculated the monthly average prices of Dated Brent and Dubai and saw that Dated was $65 and Dubai was $62; he was right about the spread not moving. However, he was wrong about this keeping him safe from losses. When he does his calculations he sees that he is losing millions. Here are his prices (Table 8.4):

This kind of result was obvious. It could have been worse or it could have been much better. The trader was simply outright long after loading and pricing his West African cargo. If Dubai had dropped to $50, he would have been in big trouble even if Brent had dropped to $40 (i.e., the Brent–Dubai spread moved to −$10). Once the purchase price was calculated, it was no longer a Brent price, it was just a fixed price and all the risk now moved to the

Table 8.4 Table of prices and P&L for crude deal into West Africa

FOB West Africa	$72/bbl	(Dated Brent + $2)
CIF Shanghai	$70.50/bbl	(Dubai + $8.50)
Freight costs	$2.00/bbl	
Net P&L	−$3.50/bbl or −$3,500,000	

Dubai market. Well, this is obviously not a great way to trade so the trader should have done some more hedging.

This time the trader realizes that the buying price and the selling price can be different because the markets are different (Brent vs. Dubai) and because the timing is different (5 days after B/L vs. the month of October). So the trader has a spread risk again. This time it is the difference between Dated Brent over the five days after loading and Dubai over the average of October. The hedge will be just like the first hedge with the Dubai swap set in October instead of the five days after the B/L date. The trader will buy a Dated Brent swap for his purchase pricing and sell a Dubai swap for the month of October. Whatever the spread is between those two swaps will determine the P&L of the deal at the moment the swaps are done. I will let you make up your own calculations, but the results should be the same as the other results if you use the same prices for Dated and Dubai as you did in all the other exercises; whatever spread you set between the swaps determines the P&L.

The difference here, other than the deal being CIF instead of FOB, is that the trader carries the hedged position for a longer time. In the first case (back-to-back dates for the pricing), the positions (physical prices and swaps) were closed once the fifth and final price was known a mere five days after loading. In the second case, the position exists until the very last day of October. There should be no extra risk, of course, but the position is slowly winding down. Let's look at how this works.

The trader buys a Brent–Dubai spread, but this time the spread is measuring the difference in price between the five day cargo pricing period and the month of October. The spread will be the difference in price between Dated Brent over five days versus Dubai over the entire month. Buying this spread is the same as buying a Dated Brent swap and selling a Dubai swap; it is exactly the same from a pricing point of view. So we can consider that the trader is long a Brent swap and is short a Dubai swap. The trader locks in the spread at $3 by buying a five day Dated Brent swap at $70 and selling an October Dubai swap at $67.

Before the first day of pricing, the trader is short the Brent–Dubai spread on their physical position (check this with your Smiley Faces, etc.) and long the Brent–Dubai spread on their swap position. This makes him flat the spread, which is what he wanted. I won't work through all the prices for this exercise but invite you to do so on your own. If your hedge doesn't work, go back and check your math and your Smiley Faces.

As the cargo starts to price in (during the five days following the B/L), the trader starts getting longer physical oil until he is long one million barrels. At the same time, his Dated Brent swap is "disappearing" as it prices in. He is buying 200,000 bbl of physical oil each day and selling 200,000 bbl of swap each day. At the end of the five days, the swap is finished and the trader is left with a long physical position. What about the Dubai swap? The trader was short the Dubai swap as part of the East–West spread trade. Is that still a position?

The Dubai swap will settle against the average Platts prices for Dubai during the month of October. Since the cargo loaded at the end of August, the swap won't start pricing for another month. So the trader is still short one million barrels of Platts Dubai pricing. So far the positions look like this (Table 8.5):

The trader no longer has any Dated Brent price risk. He is long a physical cargo of crude oil that he bought at a fixed price (whatever price he locked in using the Dated Brent swap). Against that physical length, he is still short a Dubai swap for the month of October. So his position after his purchase pricing is finished is:

Physical cargo: long 1 million barrels at a fixed price
Swap: short 1 million barrels of October Dubai

It no longer matters how fast or how slow the vessel goes. Even if it sinks or is taken by pirates, the contract pricing and the hedging are locked in. The physical oil will be sold to the Chinese over the average of October. So the trader will be getting less and less long on his physical cargo as each daily price is printed by Platts. At the same time, his swap will be getting less and less short as it is settled over the course of the month. Recall that buying or

Table 8.5 Daily positions and change in positions on crude oil arbitrage deal into Asia

Before the cargo starts pricing the position is flat
    Physical cargo: no position
    Dated Brent swap: long 1 million bbl
    Dubai swap: short 1 million bbl

	Day 1	Day 2	Day 3	Day 4	Day 5
Physical cargo					
Daily Charge	+200kb	+200kb	+200kb	+200kb	+200kb
End of day	+200kb	+400kb	+600kb	+800kb	+1000kb

The trader is long 1 million barrels of physical oil at the end of pricing.

Dated Brent Swap (long 1 million bbl)					
Daily change	-200kb	-200kb	-200kb	-200kb	-200kb
End of day	+800kb	+600kb	+400kb	+200k	Zero

selling a cargo over an average period is the same as buying and selling equal parts of that cargo individually on each day; the same math and logic apply to swaps. At mid-month, the trader will be long 500,000 bbl of physical oil and short 500,000 bbl of swap. At the end of the month he will have a fixed price for his cargo sale and a fixed price for the settlement of his swap and his position will be completely closed.

We have seen that swaps can be traded on various dates and for different sizes. They can be bought or sold for periods as far out as five years, perhaps more. The underlying commodity can be a crude oil price, a product price, or even a spread between two different commodities. If you still struggling with the mechanics of swaps (trust me, this stuff does not become second nature until you have done a bunch of trades and managed your hedging yourself), go back to the idea of a "bet" on prices and always have your Smiley Face and Frowny Face diagrams handy.

9

Futures Contracts and Forward Contracts

9.1 The Basics of Futures Contracts

Futures are considered the simplest of derivatives but are as misunderstood as swaps or any other derivative. Futures contracts are probably not even really derivatives since they are almost all physical contracts. The major exception is ICE Brent which is not a physical contract.[1] So what is a futures contract?

A futures contract is a standardized contract to buy and sell oil for delivery at a defined time and place in the future. The contract is traded on a regulated exchange in specific sizes and under specific terms and conditions. The counterparty to the trade is the clearing house of the exchange (it's okay to just say that it's the exchange and ignore the pedants who insist it is the "clearing house"). A futures exchange has rules about who can trade and how much they can trade. Deals can only be executed by approved members of the exchange. If a trader wants to buy futures, he must engage a broker who has an arrangement with a member or an owner of the exchange. Exchange-traded contracts are the "opposite" of OTC (over-the-counter) contracts. Exchanges are heavily regulated by the various financial and legal authorities in the jurisdiction of the exchange.

---

[1] For a variety of reasons no company (Shell would have been the logical choice) wanted to be responsible for organizing physical deliveries under the Brent futures contract. Brent futures are financially settled. If you buy 1 lot of Brent at $100 and the settlement price is $101, you will receive $1000 without mucking about with cargoes and loadings. The settlement price is not the final traded price, though; it is calculated based on physical market prices for North Sea crude oil.

© The Author(s), under exclusive license to Springer Nature
Switzerland AG 2023
C. Heilpern, *Understanding Risk Management and Hedging in Oil Trading*,
https://doi.org/10.1007/978-3-031-44465-4_9

The origins of futures contracts date back to early eighteenth-century Japan when the Osaka Dojima Rice Futures Exchange was officially established. Forward contracts had already existed, possibly for thousands of years, but Dojima was the first true exchange with trading hours, a ring, and standardized contracts. Dojima finally closed in June 2022 after nearly 300 years of trading.

A futures contract is a fixed price deal for delivery of a commodity at a later date. We'll stick to using oil since this book is aimed at those working in the oil industry. Let's take a simple example to show how a futures contract works. Let's buy one contract (or one lot) of NYMEX WTI. (NYMEX is the New York Mercantile Exchange which is now owned by the CME or Chicago Mercantile Exchange. The contract is also called Light Sweet Crude Oil futures.) We can't buy it directly from the exchange, so we use a broker who has an account with one of the exchange owners, i.e., someone who has a seat on the exchange. These days the trade is usually done on an electronic platform; we point and click at an app on our screen.

One lot (one contract) of WTI is 1000 bbl. We cannot call our broker and tell him we want only 780 bbl; it is 1000 bbl or nothing. If we want more, we can buy two lots, three lots, and so on. When we consider the size of a typical crude oil cargo, 1000 bbl is not very much. We are dealing with fairly fine granularity here, practically retail size contracts (a typical tanker truck carries 200 bbl of oil products).

The price of the futures contract is not negotiable. When we check the market, by looking at our Reuters, Bloomberg, or trading application screen, we see an offer price and a bid price. If we want to buy, we "lift the offer" and buy at the lowest offer price shown in the market. If we want to sell, we "hit the bid" and sell at the highest bid price shown in the market. If we don't like either price, we can put in our own prices. If we want to pay less than what is being offered, we can put in a bid below that price. For example, the market might look like this (Table 9.1):

If we want to buy a December 2025 futures contract (one lot of Dec 25), we must "lift the offer" at 67.47 which is the lowest offer price in the market. There are certainly other offers at higher levels, but we are not allowed to pay those prices (e.g., 67.48, 67.49…0.68.53, 68.54, etc.) until all the offers at 67.47 have been satisfied. We might see only 15 lots being offered at 67.47

Table 9.1 Example of futures market screen with bid and offer for crude oil futures

Contract month	Bid volume	Bid price	Offer price	Offer volume	Last trade
December 2025	7 lots	67.45	67.47	15 lots	67.47

and might assume that if we wanted to buy 100 lots, we would have to start paying more than 67.47. This is not necessarily the case since it is possible that there are many more lots on offer at 67.47 which are hidden by the sellers. We might find that even though there appears to be only a small amount on offer, it is just the tip of a large iceberg of offers from the same seller (through the exchange, of course) or other sellers. If we don't like the price of 67.47, we can choose to bid a lower price and wait to see if the market drops.

Suppose we think that 67.47 is too high. We can put in our own bid at 67.46 or lower, as low as we like. We can bid for one lot at 37.00 $/bbl just in case there is another crash like in May 2020! We cannot bid higher or at the same price as the offer in the market. We can't call up the exchange and ask if they could meet us halfway at 67.465. First of all, there is no one to talk to other than a computer program; the exchange is offering 67.47 because the exchange has a client who is offering that and that client is anonymous. Second, the price of one lot is posted and traded in dollars and whole cents only; half a cent is not possible.

I gave an example of what the screen might look using the December 2025 contract. "December 2025" is the "tenor" of the contract. Futures contracts typically list their contracts by month. In the case of Nymex, the exchange lists monthly contracts going out for ten years plus two months. If we buy a Dec 25 contract, we will be getting delivery of our WTI crude oil during the month of December 2025. So, a Nymex WTI futures contract is a physical contract with real oil being delivered if we hold onto the contract. It is not really a derivative though it is used mostly as a hedging or speculating tool with traders interested only in the price of the contract and not the physical delivery at the end. Again, if we buy Dec 25 WTI, we will get 1000 barrels delivered some time during the month of December 2025. The exact delivery dates will be agreed with the party making delivery and are subject to the rules and contract of the exchange. This means that we can't buy a Dec 25 futures contract with a delivery clause other than the whole month of December 2025.

We can use futures to make or take delivery of physical oil buy by buying or selling and holding onto the contracts until they expire. Expiry means the contracts are no longer traded on the exchange and are instead settled by physical delivery. Our Dec 25 contract would have to be held until about the 20th of November 2025 when the Dec 25 contract expires. Notice that the Dec contract expires in November and not at the end of December. This allows the exchange and anyone with an open contract to organize the physical delivery which could take place as early as the 1st of December. This is why we call it a "December" futures contract; it is for delivery in December. If the contract expired at the end of December it would mean making deliveries in January and that is not what "tenor" describes for futures.

So far we have seen that the price is not negotiable (take or leave it…or make your own bids and offers), the delivery period is not negotiable, and the size of the contract is not negotiable. Is there anything that is negotiable? No. The remaining key elements of this futures contract are the delivery location and the quality of the crude oil.

WTI futures are delivered in Cushing, Oklahoma which is a major storage and pipeline hub about 1300 kilometers from the US Gulf Coast. If you like the price of WTI futures because it is cheap compared to the price of the oil you usually buy delivered into your refinery in Singapore, you can buy WTI and take delivery but you will need to ship the oil from Cushing to Singapore by yourself. The delivery point is fixed.

This leaves the quality of the oil under the contract. We own one lot of futures which means we will be taking delivery of 1000 bbl in Dec 25. What will we get? Very simply, we will get the quality that is described by the Nymex WTI contract. The Nymex WTI specifications are fairly simple so there is really no guaranty of the exact crude we will get. It probably won't even be West Texas Intermediate but will instead be a blend of regional crudes and perhaps some shale oil. Whatever the composition, it has to match the specifications set out by Nymex which include things like a sulfur limit of 0.42% and a density of 37 API minimum and 42 API maximum.

These are the main elements of a futures contract:

Counterparty: the exchange or the exchange's clearing house
Price: fixed price which can be accepted (lift or hit) or a new/bid offer entered
Lot size: fixed by the exchange (1000 bbl in the case of Nymex WTI)
Delivery period: set by the exchange and typically during a calendar month
Quality: as per specific limits or grades. Some contracts allow multiple grades.
Delivery place: defined by the exchange, usually one port or place

The rest of the contract covers things like margins, payments, Force Majeure, and the rest. All the sorts of things we find in any oil contract for the most part.

Futures contracts move up and down with the market; they float. In fact, price discovery for oil markets begins with futures. WTI and Brent prices are the ultimate reference prices for the entire global oil market. While each quality of crude oil and oil products can have prices that move differently from Brent or WTI (these prices might go up faster than crude or go up even if crude goes down, for example), the market looks to these two futures contracts for guidance on setting the tone if not the outright level of the oil market. This might seem perverse since many people consider futures to be derivatives; this is a case of the tail wagging the dog as the derivative sets the price for the underlying commodity. Much of this seeming paradox has arisen from the financialization of the oil market. Significant percentages of futures contracts are traded by investors and speculators rather than by physical buyers and sellers looking for either physical deliveries or hedging.

Since futures prices float and since futures are so fundamental to oil prices in general, oil futures make a good hedging tool. In this case, we should treat them like derivatives. In order to do so, we have to avoid physical delivery. Crude oil futures, at least WTI and Brent, are very liquid and active. If we buy one lot, we are almost guaranteed to be able to resell that lot prior to expiry and prior to being forced to take delivery of crude oil at Cushing, OK. Since we are buying and selling from the exchange itself, when we buy and then sell, the contracts simply cancel each other out. This is different from our earlier discussions of back-to-back deals. This time the buyer, seller, and contract terms are strictly identical. The only thing that changes (or might change) is the price.

If we buy one lot of Dec 25 WTI at 67.47, we can later sell it back at the market price. If the market has gone up, we can sell higher and make a profit (Quick! According to the Smiley/Frowny diagrams, were we long or short?). If the market drops, we sell back at a loss. The market could go up and down before reaching 67.47 again, where we fortuitously sell our lot. If we don't resell though, we will take delivery of 1000 bbl of light sweet crude at 67.47, and the market might be at $25 or $125 when we get the oil. This change in price in line with the market is just like the Platts prices we used in our swap or in our offsetting physical trades we used as hedges. This means we can also hedge with futures.

9.2 Hedging Physical Oil with Futures: US Crude and WTI Futures

Suppose we own (bought at a fixed price) 200,000 bbl of crude oil in a tank in Houston, TX and have sold it for delivery in October 2025 using the average Platts prices for WTI Cargoes FOB US Gulf during that same month. Since we are long, we might lose money if the market falls. A glance at our Smiley/

Frowny faces tells us we need to hedge by selling something. WTI futures are not the same thing as Platts FOB Gulf prices, but WTI futures are very liquid and easy to trade. Traders often prefer these features and will accept or seek the basis risk that goes with using WTI futures to hedge other grades and locations of crude oil. We decide to sell 200 lots of WTI futures, but which ones?

We will be pricing our physical oil in October 2025 so we really need to protect ourselves from drops in those specific prices. Suppose we decide to sell Oct 25 WTI futures. Unfortunately, that contract will, as we know, expire before the month of October 2025. Even the Nov 25 contract will expire around the 20th of October which leaves the last third of the calendar month without a hedge. Although we can still use Nov 25 futures to hedge the first twenty days of October 2025, we need to use the Dec 25 contract to hedge the last ten days. Of course, we could take the simple route of using all Dec 25 and avoiding having to calculate the exact proportion of Nov and Dec we need to sell (based on how many Platts pricing days there are in October 2025 versus the expiry date of the Nov 25 futures contract). Let's take the simple solution and sell 200 Dec 25 futures at 61.12 USD/bbl.

By choosing December futures as our hedging tool, we avoid having the hedge price out or expire too soon. If we hedged with October futures, they would expire on the 20th of September which would leave us long the physical and unhedged. Additionally, if we forgot to buy the futures back, we could find ourselves having to make a physical delivery of crude oil in Cushing, Oklahoma! Trading December futures, which expire long after we have finished pricing our physical sale, allows us to exit our hedge without creating new risks or making new physical deliveries.

So now we are long 200,000 bbl of physical crude oil in our tank. We are short 200 lots of WTI futures. Therefore, we are flat since we have hedged. If the Nymex crude oil market drops by $20/bbl, it is likely that FOB cargoes in the Gulf will drop by very close to that amount but probably not that exact amount. We know that because the underlying oil that is represented by the Platts WTI FOB Gulf price is not the same as the underlying oil on the Nymex WTI futures contract; there is a basis risk. Those two prices might not move in perfect lock-step. If WTI futures go up by $10, FOB Gulf cargoes might only go up by $9.90. There have been times where the WTI futures price has "disconnected" from physical markets both nearby (in tank and in the pipeline) and far away (FOB on the Gulf Coast or in the North Sea) by more than $30 per barrel, so the basis risk is not negligible. WTI futures are nonetheless a common and trusted hedging tool.

9.3 How are Futures and Swaps Different When Used to Hedge?

We now run into some differences between using futures and swaps to hedge our positions. When we hedged a monthly Platts pricing using a swap, we learned that the swap automatically "disappeared"; if we bought a swap, it was automatically sold over the monthly average without our having to give instructions or sell orders. When we aligned two physical deals, one a buy and the other a sell, using the same Platts pricing days, the prices canceled each other out automatically. When we aligned a physical deal priced using Platts prices and a swap using the same Platts prices, the prices canceled each other out. We did not have to do anything more. Futures do not work that way.

When you buy a futures contract, you have two choices: you can sell it back to the exchange or you can hold onto the contract until expiry and take physical delivery. This means that any futures which are being used as a hedge do not automatically adjust to the physical position. The futures contracts will all expire on the same day. If you want to adjust your hedge, you must do it by passing an order to buy or sell lots on the exchange.

The futures position must be managed manually, though this could include programming your software to execute certain trades every day. For simplicity's sake, let's assume that we are trading manually and would need to click on our trading screen every time we wanted to buy or sell futures. (In the old days, when I was first trading, we had to call a floor broker and give orders in a now lost jargon. "Buy me a pony of Red Dec at market." That means buy me fifteen lots of the second December contract on the board at whatever price is being offered for all of those lots.)

If we assume there are twenty working days in October 2025, our physical cargo sale will price out (get a fixed price each day) 10,000 bbl every day. The positions would look similar to those we worked on when we used swaps. Here is a sample of the first three days of October 2025:

Before 4:30 pm on the 1st of October, we are long 200k bbl of physical crude oil in our tank and short 200 lots of Dec 25 WTI futures, so we are flat. If we do nothing with our futures until after October 2025, our position looks like this (kb = 1000 barrels) (Table 9.2):

As you can guess, the position keeps getting shorter and shorter every day until the end of the month when the physical cargo is sold and only the short futures position is left. This is obviously not the right way to hedge. Since the futures don't unhedge automatically, we need to do it ourselves. Once again, we need to think about what we are hedging in order to make

Table 9.2 Example of physical and hedging positions for a crude oil cargo

	1st Oct	2nd Oct	3rd Oct
Physical Cargo			
Position at start of day	+200 kb	+190 kb	+180 kb
Change of position	−10 kb	−10 kb	−10 kb
Position at end of day	+190 kb	+180 kb	+170 kb
Hedge (futures contracts)			
Position at start of day	−200 kb	−200 kb	−200 kb
Change of position	0 kb	0 kb	0 kb
Position at end of day	−200 kb	−200 kb	−200 kb
Net Position (physical + hedge)			
Position at start of day	0 kb	−10 kb	−20 kb
Change of position	−10 kb + 0	−10 kb + 0	−10 kb + 0
Position at end of day	−10 kb	−20 kb	−30 kb

the right decision on buying back our lots. The hedge was put on to protect ourselves from a drop in specific Platts prices so we need to think about how and when Platts prices are made.

We have already taken a look at the Platts window and how it works. Platts assesses prices in each of the main markets (the Americas, Europe and Africa, and East of Suez) by taking a snapshot of the markets in New York, London, and Singapore at 4:30 p.m. Our cargo is being sold in the US Gulf Coast using a Platts price that refers to the US Gulf Coast, but whatever time zone Houston is compared to New York, the Platts price for WTI in Houston is assessed at 4:30 p.m. NY time. If we are hedging, we are worried about the market price for oil at 4:30 p.m. NY time.

We need to unhedge our position manually every day at 4:30 p.m. New York time. Since we are getting short by 10 kb every day, we need to buy back 10 kb of our hedge every day. 10,000 barrels is equivalent to ten lots of WTI futures (10 lots × 1000 bbl per lot). We put an order into our broker and tell him to buy ten lots of Dec 25 at Market on Close (The market doesn't really close, so we could tell him to buy the settlement.) Or we could click on the screen ourselves at 4:30. Every day during October for which there is a Platts price, we buy back 10 lots of WTI. By the end of the month we will have bought back our entire hedge and kept a flat position during the entire month.

Futures are highly liquid, and the exchange is open nearly 24 hours a day. If the trade is small, and ten lots are very small, and the tenor is either not too far into the future or in a commonly traded tenor far down the board (December contracts are very liquid out to three or even five years), it is pretty easy to trade at almost any time of day. This is true for Brent and WTI but this would not apply to DME Oman, ICE Murban[2], and Shanghai Crude. Those markets are illiquid except for during the Platts window. If the position is not a nice, round number like 200,000 bbl but is instead 211,532 bbl, it is much easier to handle this hedge with futures whose lot size is 1000 bbl instead of a standard swap of 50,000 bbl. It is true that today's markets make it much easier to trade odd sized swaps, but there is no guaranty that you could find a seller of 37,000 or 6000 bbl of WTI swaps when you need to adjust your position (e.g., when you get the final bill of lading quantity or out-turn quantity). Even during the Platts window, a period of typically high liquidity for swaps, most of the trading is in standard sizes of 50,000 bbl or 5000 mt; finding an odd-lot seller would mean losing time and possibly losing out on the market price if the market is volatile.

9.4 Where Do the Prices of Futures Come From? What Do They Mean?

Now that we understand what futures are, let's talk about the price of futures. In all the examples and explanations so far, we took the prices for granted or just made them up. We defined futures as being fixed price trades with bids and offers but no negotiating. We said futures had tenors, usually a calendar month, for delivering the underlying oil, which give the names to each contract (July 21, Aug 22, Sep 23, Dec 25, etc.). We did not explain the relationship between the market price today, what we would call the "spot market," the tenor of the contracts and the prices of those futures contracts. Let's start by saying what the price of a futures contract isn't:

> The price of a futures contract is not a prediction of where the price of oil will be in the future.
> A futures contract does not tell you where the price of oil will be in the future.
> Futures prices don't give predictions of where oil prices will be in the future.

---

[2] Murban trades on ICE Futures Abu Dhabi or IFAD. It is a physical delivery contract for Murban crude oil loading FOB Fujairah. Since Fujairah is outside the Arab Gulf, this makes the contract more appealing than if it were delivered inside the politically and militarily volatile Arab Gulf. Freight costs are also lower versus loading from Abu Dhabi.

I said this three times in slightly different ways because the concept is hard for many people to accept. Most people, including many people in the oil business, believe that futures markets tell you where prices will be, that futures prices are predictions or estimates of prices in the future. This is demonstrably false as shown by many statistical studies by business school students, oil analysts, and investment banks, including JP Morgan. People don't believe this because they hear on CNBC or Bloomberg that analysts and traders are predicting higher prices because the contracts for one year from today rose by $1 or they are higher than the price of spot oil. I won't reproduce the JP Morgan or other studies here, but invite you to do some of your own research. Instead, I will go back to the definition of what a futures contract is once again.

A futures contract is a deal done today at a fixed price for delivery of oil in the future. There is no uncertainty about the price; it is fixed the instant you do the deal. It will not be set later; it is set right now. The "future" part of a futures contract is the delivery. The deal is agreed today for a delivery some time in the future. Nowhere in this definition or in the mechanics of futures is there any mention of prediction or guessing at future values. Anyone who looks at the ICE Brent screen for a few days in a row can easily see that the prices change every day, even every second. If the price of the Dec 22 futures contract is 62.11 $/bbl today and futures predict where the market will be in the future, how can you explain that the next day the same futures contract is being traded at 57.38 $/bbl. All Dec 22 contracts are identical except for the price. So if futures predict the price in the future, they can't really make up their mind. Take a look at the futures prices back in mid 2008. The price for Dec 08 WTI was close to $140. A few months later, Dec 2008 was at $30. If this is a prediction, it is much worse than a coin toss. If these prices are not predictions, what are they?

Futures prices (the prices for futures contracts) are the prices agreed right now for delivery later. The point of time when you get something has a definite effect on its value and therefore changes the price you are willing to pay for it. Having something in your hand now instead of later might be worth quite a bit to you. Or, you might not want to or cannot take delivery right now, but are willing to pay for a later delivery at a higher price.

9.5 Elephants and Bottles of Water: Explaining Contango and Backwardation

Suppose you own an elephant. It is a friendly elephant and almost housebroken. You like your elephant but you live in a two bedroom apartment, one room for you and one for Jumbo, which is a bit expensive. You would like to move into a smaller place and save $100 a month in rent, but that means selling the elephant. You place an add in the local paper to sell Jumbo for $1000, a fair price for an African bull elephant on the London market. An elephant enthusiast calls you right away and agrees to the price. Unfortunately, he can't take Jumbo right away as he needs to decorate the spare bedroom first so Jumbo will feel at home. He tells you he will take delivery in three months. You like this buyer since he really seems to care about elephants, but the three month delay is a problem. It costs you money to hold onto Jumbo.

Every month you keep Jumbo you need to pay rent for the bigger apartment. You have to buy Elephant Chow and spend hours cleaning up his room. There are veterinary bills and renter's insurance as well as the occasional broken door and wall. Each month of waiting to get rid of Jumbo costs you $150 ($100 in rent and $50 in food, bills, etc.). You tell the buyer that if he takes Jumbo today, he can have him for $1000; if he agrees to the deal today but only picks him up in three months, the price is $1450. The extra $450 is to cover your costs of keeping the elephant for three more months.

What does this tell us about the market price of elephants in three months? Nothing really. The prices being discussed are for a deal done today, not a deal whose price will be negotiated in three months. If the usual price for an elephant is $1000 at the pet store, then it is likely that the market price for elephants will be $1000 in three months. If suddenly there are fewer elephants available, the spot price might be $3000 in three months. Or if a fresh shipment arrives in a few months, the elephant market might collapse down to $500.[3] But as a seller, you can choose to sell for delivery right now or for later delivery. If choose the latter, you have to pay the cost of holding onto the elephant until delivery is made. As a buyer, you can take delivery now; if you choose to buy today but take delivery later, you will have to compensate the seller for his costs. Some of you might say, "Well, if the price is likely to be $1000 in three months, then the buyer should just wait and buy in the spot market in three months." I pointed out that the price for elephants might

---

[3] I do not advocate the buying and selling of elephants or keeping them as pets or in zoos. I think that this analogy is useful, though, and further state that no elephants were harmed in the making of this book.

change, and the buyer might discover that elephants are very expensive in three months or that there is a shortage and he will have to wait another three months and pay an even higher price. The buyer might really like Jumbo and want to guaranty that he will get him in three months.

This market situation is called "contango." Contango is a situation where prices for delivery today are cheaper than prices for delivery tomorrow. Or prices for delivery in six months are cheaper than prices for delivery in seven months. In this case, the market for elephants is in contango; it is cheaper to do a deal for prompt delivery than to do a deal for delivery in three months. Contango is explained by economists as the cost of storage; when a deal is concluded today at a fixed price but delivery is later, the seller is essentially storing the oil (or elephant) for the client. The storage cost is built into the price for later delivery.

Now let's look at the other possibility. Suppose the prices for later delivery were lower than those for prompt delivery. If you want your stuff right now, it has a premium associated with it. If you are willing to wait, you get a discount. Most of us are aware of express shipping when we buy something online. If we pay the regular price, our novelty coffee mugs will arrive in two weeks. If we pay an extra $14, we can get them in two days. This clearly shows that delivery, earlier or later, has a value. For coffee mugs, it might be getting them delivered in time for someone's birthday. In oil and other commodities, it could be something more fundamental and crucial.

Suppose you are wandering lost in the desert. You are dying of thirst, as one tends to do when lost in the desert. You come across Trader Bob's Bottled Water Company. Bob greets you effusively and offers to sell you a chilled bottle of spring water. It certainly looks wonderfully refreshing and frankly life-saving. You ask him how much for a bottle and he tells you $1000 per bottle, limit three per customer. You are a bit shocked and ask him if he doesn't have something cheaper, perhaps not as chilled or maybe a generic brand. Bob tells you he can certainly offer you something cheaper and asks if you would like to buy the same brand of water in the same size bottle and chilled to the same pleasant temperature but for a bargain price of only $10. This seems like a reasonable price for a bottle of water in the middle of the desert and you are, after all, dying of thirst, so you agree. Bob congratulates you on your economic intelligence and says he will get your bottle for you but you have to wait a bit. You ask him how long you need to wait, and Bob tells you, "One week."

Now, you can camp out in the shade of Bob's porch and try to wait one week, but it won't be pleasant. As you are trying to decide which water to buy, a busload of American tourists pull up. They, too, are lost. They, too, are dying of thirst. They pile into Bob's shop and start shouting and waving credit cards around. Not many are interested in waiting one week. Most seem to have plenty of money and one immediately snaps up three bottles at $1000 a piece. The next buyer bids $1100, then another bids $1200, and soon a bottle of Bob's water for immediate delivery is being sold at $1800. Finally, there is one bottle left. If you change your mind and decide you are so thirsty that you can't wait a week, you would have to buy a prompt bottle for at least $1800.

This kind of market is called a backwardated market. Backwardation is when prices for prompt delivery are higher than prices for later delivery. Economists understand contango; the higher costs for later delivery reflect the cost of storing and holding the commodity. For backwardation, they had a harder time explaining and finally settled on something they call "convenience yield." Convenience yield is the benefit a buyer or holder of a commodity gets by having it on hand, in stock and ready to consume. Many businesses have excess stocks of their raw materials simply because it is easier, cheaper, and more reliable to take large deliveries once or twice a month rather than rely on Just-In-Time inventory. A baker who buys only the flour he needs to make one batch of bread might discover that his supplier is closed or unable to make a delivery before the following week. The baker is ready to pay up to get an ample supply of flour delivered, perhaps enough for one week of baking. He is not willing to sell his stock of flour unless he gets a very high price because it would mean canceling all his sales and potentially losing clients for good. He gets an economic yield from the convenience of having an ample supply of flour in his store room.

Coming back to our water and tourists dying of thirst, we can probably say that they are panicking. They are willing to pay whatever price they can afford in order to get at least one bottle of water right now. If they can build up a small stock of three bottles before it is sold out, that stock will last at least until they get back to their hotel. Are they willing to pay $1000 for a bottle delivered in a week or in a month? Not likely. We don't panic about future events when faced with a disaster or impending doom. One existential crisis at a time, please. You and the tourists also assume that in a week you will be either dead or out of the desert; there is no compelling need to buy emergency water at $1000 if you won't get it for a week. Perhaps you might buy a few bottles at $10 for delivery in a week or in a month if you plan on heading back out into the desert, but you would be unlikely to pay $1000 for that water since you believe you have learned your lesson and are unlikely to get lost or run out completely next time. Locking in a few bottles at $10 that you can pick up in a month might make sense, though.

9.6 The Forward Curve

When we talk about futures markets, contango and backwardation, we are talking about market structure and the "shape of the forward curve." The forward curve of futures (or swaps and forwards) is made up of the prices of each futures contract in chronological order (i.e., earliest deliveries first). It is a graph of the prices of these contracts at a moment in time. Recall that futures prices are determined *right now*, so if we have six futures contracts which are trading nearly simultaneously, we can take a screen shot and freeze that moment in time. It might look like this (assume we are in December 2021 and "22" means the year 2022[4]) (Table 9.3):

This market is in contango; the near delivery date (Jan 22) contracts are cheaper than the farther delivery dates. In this case we would say there is a $1 per month contango. Where do you think prices will be in June of 2022? If you said 75.00, you need to reread this entire section. If you said you don't know, then you can keep reading.

If we plot the contracts and the prices, we can create a curve which is called the forward curve. For the prices above, it would look like this (Fig. 9.1):

Since we are looking at the prices for futures contracts at a split second in time, there is only one price for each contract. There are no prices other than at the dots. The first price, Jan 22, is the price for delivery of crude oil in Jan 22. There are no prices in between that price and the price for the Feb 22 contract. There are no futures contracts for delivery on the 27th of January or on the 13th of February. It is the full month or nothing. So a forward curve of futures prices is less a curve and more a collection of dots. However, since we are human beings, we instinctively and naturally connect the dots to create lines. We might commonly see the forward curve presented as follows (Fig. 9.2):

Table 9.3 Example of futures list of prices

Contract	Price (last)
Jan 22	70.00
Feb 22	71.00
Mar 22	72.00
Apr 22	73.00
May 22	74.00
Jun 22	75.00

---

[4] I started writing this book in 2020 during COVID so some of the dates are, well, out of date. This does not matter for explaining the principles involved. Hop into your mental time machine and pretend you are in December 2021 all over again.

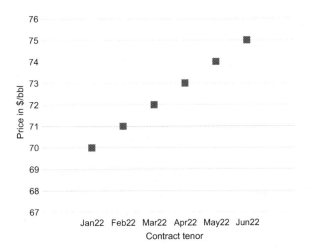

Fig. 9.1 Simple graph of the forward curve of futures prices with just the price plots

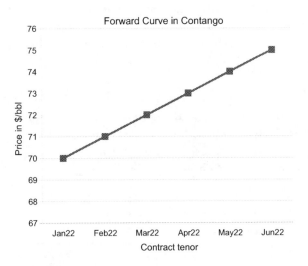

Fig. 9.2 Forward curve as a line graph

We have connected the dots but remember that the only prices that exist are the dots themselves; the line is imaginary. Our brain not only creates an imaginary line, it becomes easily tricked by this line or even by the series of dots alone. If we look at the line we see that it is rising into the future. Our brains use their simple, quick, and dirty reasoning (heuristics) and tell us that if this graph is going up, then prices are going up as well. This graph looks pretty much like an "up" arrow on a projection chart (showing profits or sales into the future, for example). Our brain sees this (Fig. 9.3):

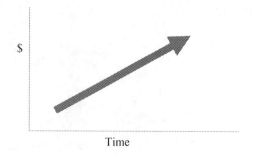

Fig. 9.3 How our brain sees a forward curve

Our brain is wrong. Futures prices do not predict prices. Futures prices are prices made RIGHT NOW for delivery in the future.

Let's look at a backwardated market (a forward curve in backwardation). The screen shot of the exchange price listing might look like this (Table 9.4):

Here, the market is backwardated by varying amounts. Indeed, a market can have different levels of backwardation or contango between the various contracts. The market can be in contango in one part of the curve and backwardated for the rest. Let's draw the forward curve for our backwardated market (Fig. 9.4):

Here the line is sloping downward, but that does not mean prices will be lower in the future. The prices in the graph are the prices made right now, in the present, for a delivery in the future. If you find that I am saying this over and over and being tedious, it is because your brain will keep trying to trick you and so will many people in the market!

Table 9.4 Price list of forward curve of futures prices

Contract	Price
Jun 23	80.00
Jul 23	79.00
Aug 23	77.50
Sept 23	76.00
Oct 23	73.00
Nov 23	70.00

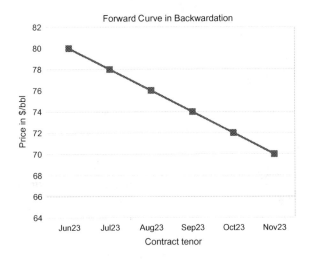

Fig. 9.4 Forward curve of a backwardated market

9.7 Do Contango and Backwardation Make Predictions About Prices?

Does market structure tell us anything about prices or give any clue to their direction? Well, the easiest answer is no because that avoids falling into the trap of believing that futures prices are predictions. The harder answer is that market structure can give us clues to the state of the spot market and where those prices are going, but not where they will be farther out in the future. Market structure can be an indicator of a bullish or bearish market, at least for spot prices.

When a market is in backwardation, this might imply that buyers are panicking or supply is short or at risk. Buyers are willing to pay up for real oil they can get right away rather than cheaper oil that may or may not show up. If there is a threat of war in the Arab Gulf, many buyers would bid up prices for cargoes that are already loaded and sailing outside the AG. They want to build up their reserves today with real oil they can use in case things heat up and the Straits of Hormuz are shut. Buyers will pay higher and higher prices as the supply of prompt oil is quickly bought up by the market. Buyers won't panic about deliveries in six months; things will probably be back to normal by then or supply flows will have changed, and they will find ample oil from some other markets. Since we (consumers, traders, reporters, Platts, and everyone else) use "market" prices to mean spot prices, it is clear that the airwaves and fiber optic cables will be buzzing with stories about how strong the market is and how it is rising every day. CNBC and CNN won't have special reports talking about how the December 2026 futures contract is stable at $58, where it has been for six months. Instead, they won't even talk about backwardation since they probably don't know what it is. They will simply report that spot oil prices are at $80 and rising, for example. Platts, whose reporters understand market structure perfectly well, will also report high market prices because they assess and report the spot market, not the prices for delivery in three months or in three years. A backwardated market is, all other things being equal, more likely to be a bullish market.

A contango market is, all things being equal, a bearish market. Oil markets are fairly inelastic[5] both for supply and demand, which is why panic can quickly create backwardation. If supply outstrips demand, producers can either shut down production or continue to produce and entice buyers to consume or store the excess oil. Contango implies overproduction which implies falling prices. Producers are having a fire sale to get rid of their excess. Producers won't discount next year's production, though, since the market might change by then; why sell cheap when you are not yet sure if you have to?

Contango curves tell our brain the market is rising but that is wrong. If anything, contango might indicate oversupply and a bearish spot market. Backwardation's declining slope tricks us into believing prices will be going lower when it is more likely to mean spot prices are bullish. Generally, the steeper the contango, the weaker the spot market. The steeper the backwardation, the stronger the spot market. By steeper, I mean that the difference in prices, especially between the front contracts, is very large.

Since swaps are similar to futures, they also have a forward curve. Some of my students who begrudgingly accept that futures don't predict prices insist that swaps do. They say that because typical oil swaps are based on Platts prices in the future, that swaps are a prediction of where prices will be. All the same arguments apply to swaps that apply to futures for why they are not predictions. Look at what Platts is to begin with. The prices published (reported, not invented) by Platts are prices agreed today (deals done during the Platts Window) for physical delivery in the future! The prices we see reported in Platts do not represent cargoes that were physically exchanged today; the deals were concluded today, but the delivery will take place in three days to a month and a half in the future depending on the specific crude oil or product. This means that Platts prices are inherently forward looking, like

---

[5] Inelastic markets are those in which supply or demand doesn't respond quickly to price changes. Oil consumption remains stable across broad price ranges. People simply need to drive to work or heat their homes. It takes large increases to cut into gasoline consumption. Conversely, when oil prices collapse, consumers don't leave their cars running overnight.

futures, even if Platts says they report spot prices. So if we buy a swap, we are buying the value of a delivery in the future as reported by Platts.

Suppose we are in June and we buy a Platts swap for 10 ppm Diesel Cargoes FOB NWE for December at $600/mt. While a swap is not a physical contract, it is based on the physical contracts which Platts uses to assess the market. So the settlement price of our swap (the market price used to see who won or lost the "bet") will be based on physical cargoes transacted during the month of December and delivered between the 10th of December and about the 25th of January. The price of the swap is determined right now in June and is calculated or determined in the same way futures prices are calculated or determined. Swaps are no more a prediction of where Platts will be in the future than futures contracts are. In fact, it is possible to buy or sell a swap which settles against the daily settlement price of futures contracts (i.e., make a "bet" on where futures contract prices will be during, say, the month of December 2025).

9.8 Forwards or Forward Contracts

What are Forward Contracts?

Much as futures are not really derivatives because they typically involve physical delivery, forwards (forward contracts) are very much physical contracts as well, though they are often used as derivatives. A forward is something like a futures contract except that it is OTC (Over The Counter) and is a physically settled contract. Forward contracts are usually large; some were originally full cargoes such as Brent (500,000 bbl) or European Flexi Cargoes (25–30,000 MT). Forwards have been used in markets where there is no adequate futures or swaps market and where there is a deep and liquid physical market of standard quality and quantity. There are not many liquid forward markets left since futures and swaps have expanded and replaced forwards as hedging tools.

A classic forward market is the North Sea crude oil forward contract, commonly called the Paper Brent (not to be confused with a Dated Brent Swap) market or the BFOET market…or even 30 Day Brent or Forward Brent, etc. The contract is a standard form where generally the only things that change are the names of the buyer and seller and the price. Otherwise, the Brent Forward Contract is for 700,000 bbl of one of five grades of crude oil (Brent, Forties, Oseberg, Ekofisk, and Troll) for loading during a calendar month. Forwards trade on a fixed price basis, which makes them useful as hedging tools. What makes them tricky as hedging tools are their size and their physical delivery.

If a trader wants to hedge a 500,000 bbl cargo with Paper Brent, he has to buy or sell a 700,000 bbl cargo, leaving a 200 kb exposure. Additionally, even if he reversed his position (e.g., bought and sold the same month forward contract), he might still end up stuck with a physical cargo under the terms of the standard contract. It is possible to buy and sell from the same counterparty and create a "washout" with no physical delivery, but this is not guaranteed going into the first deal. (For details on the Brent Forward market, please see A. Imsirovic.[6])

If forward contracts are standardized like futures and swaps, it is to make them liquid and easy to pass on. If you want to buy a cargo of diesel, you need to specify a large number of items with the seller including the price formula, the payment terms, delivery dates, type of delivery (FOB or CIF), the load port or destination, and so on. If you want to buy a Brent Forward, you can call up Phibro or Shell and ask for an offer on Sep BFOET. The trader will give you a price, which is the only thing you now have to negotiate. Everything else is standard.

Because forwards are lumpy (700,000 bbl is a big position and tricky to use as a hedge), the market has developed smaller forwards called partials. Partials allow a trader to buy or sell in chunks as small as 25,000 bbl, though 100,000 or 50,000 bbl trades are more common. In addition to being more manageable, the partials don't lead to physical delivery, unless a certain minimum quantity has been accumulated with the same counterparty. Partials have grown in popularity and greatly increased liquidity in the remaining liquid forward markets, Brent and Dubai. In practice, the only oil markets which have enough liquidity and transparency for forwards to be used as hedges are the Brent and Dubai markets. European Flexi, Boston Bingo, and Littlebrook have all gone the way of the dodo.

Using forwards to hedge is much like using an opposite physical position except that the forward is standardized and more liquid than a physical cargo. They also trade using a fixed price as opposed to most other physical deals which use floating prices.

---

[6] See Trading and Price Discovery for Crude Oils, A. Imsirovic as well as numerous OEIS publications by the same author.

10

Options

10.1 What is an Option? A Simplified, Friendly Approach

This is not a book about understanding the math and formulae for calculating the value of options. I don't intend to explain option strategies like Straddles and Strangles. Those sorts of things are designed for trading using options and for managing the risks in an options trading book. There are hundreds of excellent books which explain option trading strategies, the Black–Scholes formula and Monte Carlo Simulations far better than I can, so I won't even try! As for learning to trade options, that is an entirely different and complex job. For that reason options have their own chapter here. Most physical traders will never trade or need to trade options, but everyone should understand the basics.

Instead of learning complex math and option strategies, we will take a look at using options as hedging tools. Specifically, we will look at Asian Options or what are also called Average Price Options, since these are the most common and useful tool for hedging oil price risk. We need to start by explaining what an option is. Most text books or trading guides say that options are financial derivatives that give buyers the right, but not the obligation, to buy or sell an underlying asset at an agreed-upon price and date (Investopedia, inter alia). Options are not common in every day life, but there are some examples that many of you have heard of.

In Hollywood we hear of movie companies optioning a book or screenplay. This means the studio has paid the author a sum of money to have the right to turn the book into a movie. The studio doesn't have to make the movie, but the author can't sell his book to anyone else until that contract expires. The studio bought an option from the author; if they decide to make the movie, the author has to let them.

Many of us buy our airline tickets online. These days it is easier and easier to book far ahead without committing to the ticket. In the old days you could buy a full fare ticket which was fully refundable. Then budget travel came along, and airlines agreed to sell cheap seats but without refunds or changes. Today, you can book flights on British Airways or Air France directly (on their web site) and pay a small fee to have the right to cancel the ticket up to a certain date. The price of ticket is determined at the moment you buy it; the price won't change. A consumer can buy an option on an airline ticket. Here is a question for you: is the consumer buying a call or a put?

Any time you make a non-refundable deposit for something, you are buying an option. If you book a ball room for your daughter's wedding and they want $500 to hold the room for you for three months, you might not get your money back if your daughter runs off to join an Ashram instead of marrying her childhood sweetheart. On the other hand, the venue can't rent the room out to anyone else for as long as they agreed to hold it for you. If the wedding goes ahead, you hire the room at the price that was agreed three months before.

All of these are examples of everyday options. We pay for the right to get or do something if we want to do it. We are under no obligation but the other side is. Now we have to figure out how this helps us hedge oil price risk.

10.2 Calls and Puts

Standard or vanilla options come in two types, Calls and Puts. A call is what I showed in those everyday examples. The buyer of a call pays a premium (or non-refundable deposit in everyday terms) for the right to buy oil or a derivative at the agreed price. The buyer of a put pays a premium for the right to sell oil or a derivative at an agreed price. The oil or derivative that can be bought or sold at the agreed price is the underlying of the option. The premium is the price of the option. The agreed price is called the strike price of the option.

If a trader buys an $80 call for a cargo of crude oil, he now has the right to call up the seller of the option and ask him for a physical delivery as per the terms of the contract. He can call up the option seller and force him to sell him a cargo of crude oil at $80. When will the trader call up and "exercise" the option, which is to say tell the option seller that he is taking delivery of the oil and paying $80 for it? Logically, the trader would only exercise the option if the spot market is higher than $80. If the spot market is at $70 and the trader wants a cargo of crude, he can buy it from the market at $70. He is under no obligation to call up the option seller if he doesn't want to. If the market goes up to $90, the trader still has no obligation to call the option seller, though it might be foolish not to. If the market is at $90, the trader can exercise the option and buy a cargo at $80. The option seller (who we say "wrote the option") has no choice once the option deal is concluded; if the trader wants to take delivery under the option contract (exercise the option), the option seller must comply whether the market is at $70, $90 or $150.

If a trader buys a $60 put for a cargo of crude oil, he now has the right to call up the option seller and make him buy a cargo at $60, the strike price of the option. He probably won't do this if the market is over $60 since he can get a higher price by selling into the market instead. He would likely exercise the option if the market drops below $60. In that case, he can exercise the option and sell the cargo to the seller of the put at agreed price of $60. The seller of the put must buy the cargo at $60 if the trader exercises the option no matter what the market price might be.

Using options like this for physical deliveries is rare. Most options traders do not trade physical oil and would not know what to do with a cargo or perhaps are not even allowed to trade physical oil. This is the case for most oil traders who work at banks. Instead, most options are used to deliver either futures contracts, in the case of options on Nymex WTI or ICE Brent, or to deliver prices like a classical derivative (e.g., a swap).

What benefit did the trader who bought the $80 call get? Let's say he was short a cargo of crude oil that he sold at $75 fixed price. He is bearish and expects to be able to cover his short (buy a cargo of crude oil) at below $75, perhaps as low as $60. Of course, he knows that he can't predict prices, but only make an expert guess at the trend in the market. If OPEC suddenly announces a 25% cut, oil will shoot up and the trader might end up paying $100 for the cargo, creating a fairly catastrophic loss. He calculates that he can afford to lose no more than $5 a barrel on this deal before he risks getting into too deep a hole or even getting fired. He needs some sort of insurance to prevent catastrophic loss. The $80 call means that if the market goes above $80, he can still pay only $80 by exercising the option. By owning the $80 call option, he has limited his loss to $5 a barrel (buy at $80 using the option and sell at $75 into his short position).

What about the trader who bought the $60 put. In this case, suppose the trader owned a cargo of oil that he bought at $65 which he intended to sell into the market in the future. If the market collapses, he might be forced to sell at $35 and get fired, divorced, etc. Since he bought the $60 put, he can always call up the option seller and make him take the cargo at $60. His loss is limited to $5 a barrel.

Buying options in both these cases limits the trader's loss to $5 a barrel. His profit, on the other hand, is "limitless." For the trader who bought the call, he has no obligation to exercise it. If the market drops to $15 a barrel, he can throw away the option contract and buy a spot cargo on the market at $15. For the trader who bought the put, he can ignore it as well. If the market rises to $200 a barrel, he can sell into the market and never bother to call the person who sold him the put.

The trader who bought the call had a physical position. He was short a cargo of crude oil at $75. If you check the Smiley/Frowny face diagrams, you will see that he would be unhappy if prices rose. He would be happy if prices fell. Hedging means neutralizing the Frowny face. The call option does that. In the examples we are using, the trader bought a call which could allow a $5 loss, but the loss cannot be higher than that. If the trader had bought a $75 call, he could have limited his loss to break-even while leaving the Smiley intact.

The trader who bought the put also had a physical position. He was long a cargo at $65. His Frowny face is caused by prices going down. His $60 put option means the Frowny face disappears at that price. If he has bought a $65 put, he would have neutralized his Frowny face entirely and left his Smiley face.

10.3 "Half a Swap": Hedging with Options

When we used swaps to hedge our positions, we saw that in order to get rid of the Frowny face, we had to accept to get rid of the Smiley face. Our positions became flat overall. The price of the swap (e.g., $600 December Mean of Platts Diesel Swap) locked in the P&L of the positions. Recall that we described a swap as a "bet" on where prices would go. Well, we can win a bet, but we can also lose it. The swap has upside and downside. Ideally, we would like to enter into a swap that pays us off if we are right (protects us against adverse price movements) but which we can ignore if we lose the bet (the market moves in the direction that makes us happy). Imagine making bets at the black jack table in Vegas and never having to lose your chips when you bust or the dealer beats your hand. What we really want from our hedging is half a swap, the good half.

If you think about the calls and puts we described, you will see that they are simply half a swap. The call option pays you if the market goes up, but you don't lose anything if the market goes down. The put option pays you if the market falls, but you don't lose anything if the market rises. It sounds like the perfect free lunch.

I started this section by saying we would look primarily at Asian or Average Price Options because they are the most suited to hedging typical price exposure in oil markets. Let's define what an Asian option is.

Asian options are purely financial derivatives like swaps. The underlying of an Asian option is a price, typically the same prices that are commonly traded as swaps. So if we can trade a monthly swap for a Platts price, we should be able to trade an Asian option for that same price. Swaps are settled by calculating the average price over the period of the swap (e.g., Monthly Average of Mean of Platts Singapore 180 CST Fuel Oil). Since options are "half a swap," they are also settled by calculating the same averages. Just like the swap, the settlement of the Asian option is automatic; the buyer does not need to exercise the option, just as he does not need to exercise a swap.

10.4 Average Price Options: Asian Calls or Caps

Let's go back to our trader and his short cargo position (he sold a cargo at $75). Instead of waiting to buy in the market at a fixed price, he decides to buy at the monthly average for Dated Brent for next month. He is still short, of course, since he would be unhappy to see Dated Brent prices rise (check your Frowny faces), so he decides to buy an Asian option to protect himself. Since he is worried about rising prices, he needs to buy a call. Let's say he buys a $75 Asian call for Dated Brent for the next month from an investment bank. He will buy a cargo in the market at the monthly average price; let's say that it turns out to be $83. He loses $8 on this physical cargo. His Asian call means he can "buy" the Dated Brent price at $75 and sell it back to the bank at $83, the average price over the month. This is just like owning the good half of a swap. The bank owes him $8 a barrel. The result is as if he bought the cargo at $75, and he breaks even on his deal.

If the market price drops to $71, he pays $71 for his physical cargo and nothing happens with the option; he does not have to pay the bank. All of this is automatic, like a swap. In this case, the trader makes a profit of $4 on the physical cargo without any gain or loss on the option.

If you use a few more examples yourself, you will see that no matter how high the average Dated Brent goes over the month, the trader will never have to pay more than $75 for his oil. The option compensates him for the rise. His price is capped at $75. For this reason, Asian call options are often called "Caps."

The second trader is long and so is worried about falling prices. He decides to sell on the monthly average as well so he is still long his cargo. To protect himself against falling prices, he buys an Asian put with a strike price of $60. If the monthly average falls below $60, the bank will pay him the difference. This payment offsets the lower price he gets for his physical oil. Essentially, the option is putting a floor under his price; he will not have to sell lower than $60 when the whole position is taken into account. Asian puts are usually called "Floors."

Asian options are particularly suited to consumers and producers. An airline buys jet fuel at fixed prices every day (into planes at the airport) and is worried about spikes in prices. If the price of jet fuel rises too much, they won't be able to fill airplanes; few travelers want to fly from New York to London for $2000 in economy. If they buy swaps and the market drops, they are stuck with higher priced fuel and might not be competitive if other airlines did not hedge. If they buy a cap, they set a limit on how much they will pay for jet fuel while enjoying the windfalls if the market falls. The cap is also automatic and settled financially; they don't need to worry about exercising the option or arranging any physical deliveries.

Producers are in the opposite position, of course. If the market price collapses below their production costs, they will either lose money or be forced to cut production. If a producer buys a "floor," he can guaranty a minimum selling price as well as enjoy greater profits if the market rises. In this case the producer would be buying an Asian put.

Both producers and consumers in the oil industry tend to buy or sell on a regular basis and are exposed to pretty much the average price over the year. Asian options typically settle against a whole month average which is suitable in this case. If an airline buys a one year cap for jet at $75 a barrel, the payments will be calculated on a monthly basis (just like a swap). If the average Platts price in January is $78, the bank will send them $3 a barrel (for the volume of the option). If the February average price is $72, nothing happens. Then March average is $94 and the bank pays them $19. Even if the option covers three years, the settlements are made monthly at the end of each month during the option period.

10.5 Option Pricing…Simplified

I said earlier that this sounds like the ultimate free lunch: the good side of a bet with no obligation to pay if you lose. I also said that there is no such thing as a risk-free deal either, so you can guess that there is a catch to buying options (and selling them). The catch is that options are not free. This should be easy to understand if you think about the everyday examples I gave earlier. The non-refundable security deposit or the payment made to the author for the right to buy his screenplay are the prices to be paid to buy those options. In option trading we would call these prices "premiums." There are complex and complicated option pricing models out there which require strange symbols to write. If you become an options trader, you might need to know those formulas (like the Black–Scholes model). Here, we will just discuss the things that affect the value, and consequently the price, of an option.

When a trader buys an option, he has no risk. If the option works and pays off, he makes money. If the market goes the other way, he ignores the option and doesn't exercise it. The option buyer owns the Smiley Face side of the swap. If you buy a call option for 1 million barrels of crude oil at $85 a barrel, you have two choices: you can exercise the option or ignore it. If the market is at $70, you can buy crude in the market at $70. You would not exercise your option; you would not call up your counterparty and tell him you are going to pay him $85 a barrel when you could buy it $15 cheaper elsewhere. If the market goes up to $100, you can now call up your counterparty, exercise the option, and buy from him at $85. If the market is below $85 you buy from the market; if it's above $85, you can buy at $85 from the guy who sold you the option. It's a no-lose situation.

The seller (or writer) of the option has the opposite position; he potentially has the losing side of the swap with no Smiley Face. Think of the seller's position this way. Many of you are willing to spend a dollar or two to buy a lottery ticket, but how much would you demand if I asked you to sell ten thousand lottery tickets with prizes from one hundred to one million dollars? You would not sell the tickets for free even if the probability of someone winning was small. If you are good at math, you could calculate the odds of a winning number for each of the prizes and then the overall risk/reward. If you are bad at math, you can at least say the price of a ticket would not be zero!

An option seller has (theoretically) unlimited risk. Take the case of the cap. The bank has to compensate the option buyer for every cent the market is over $80. The market cannot really rise to infinity, but if it climbs to $150 again, that will be close enough to infinity for a banker who sold 10 million barrels of caps. Sellers of floors are perhaps less worried since, despite WTI futures hitting −$37 a barrel in April 2020, it is exceedingly improbable that a monthly average crude price would drop below zero, though perhaps fuel oil or some other price could. In any case, option sellers have only downside. To accept this and to manage their risk, they require an upfront payment, the option premium.

The price of an option (or the option premium) depends on how much buyers are willing to pay to have only the Smiley Face side of the swap and how much sellers of the option require to get them to accept the Frowny Face side of the swap. Again, there is no guaranty that the option will be exercised, so it is not certain that the seller will lose money, but there is no way he will make money either. How much would you ask for to take that kind of position? And how would calculate the premium?

I promised you that I would not delve into the math of options pricing, and so I won't. Instead I will just explain the principles that drive the value, and therefore price, of an option. Recall that options have an underlying. For some of our examples we used Dated Brent prices. Options have a strike price, the level at which the option makes money or is automatically triggered in the case of an Asian option. Options also have time limits. Asian options cover the period that is negotiated and only that period. If you buy a cap for 2023, the option starts on the 1st of January 2023 and finishes on the 31st of December 2023. If you buy a classic call or put (think of the physical cargo options I presented), they almost always have an expiry date. So the buyer of the $80 call for a physical cargo of crude oil may be allowed two months to exercise the option. If he does not exercise it within that time limit, the option expires.

Whether or not an option pays out (makes money for the buyer and costs money to the seller), depends on the market going past the strike price. If you sell a $100 call, you lose money only if the market rises above $100 (remember that the seller of a call will have to sell the oil at $100 to the option buyer if the call is exercised). If the market today for Dated Brent is $66, how likely is it that Dated Brent will go over $100 and the option will be exercised? Obviously this depends on how much crude prices go up and down (random or "stochastic" price movements) and how long you let them move. If Dated Brent prices only go up and down at most ten cents every day (We can measure price movements and calculate them as a percentage of the base price. This is called volatility.), then we would expect with a high degree of certainty that tomorrow Dated Brent will be between $65.90 and $66.10 ($66 ± 0.10 $/bbl). The odds of the $100 call being exercised within one day are very slim. However, if we give Brent prices enough time, perhaps years even, a random walk of prices going up and down by ten cents every day could move prices to over $100 and lead to the option being exercised.

So the cost of an option to a seller, the risk of potential loss, depends on how much the price jumps around and how long the option is allowed to run before it expires. The more volatile prices are and the longer they are allowed to move, the more likely they will reach the strike price (whether or not that price is above or below the market…volatility is about prices jumping up and down, not just up.) So an option seller will need a bigger premium to cover his risk when prices are volatile and the option lasts a long time. What about the strike price of the option?

Ask yourself if you would make a bet with me right now where I bet that Brent futures will be higher than $1000 within five minutes. Would you bet $100 on that? Could Brent jump to $1000 in just five minutes? Yes, theoretically, but it is very, very unlikely. If Brent is at $66 right now, would you make the same bet if we set the strike price at $66.50 instead of $1000 (i.e., you bet it won't reach $66.50)? Probably not. The farther away the strike price of the option is from the market, the less likely it is that the market will reach that price and so the option premium is lower. The option is worth less.

Think of a cap or an Asian Call. It sets the highest price a consumer will have to pay in the market. If an airline buys a cap at $100 with the jet market price at $90, it will theoretically never pay more than $100 for its jet fuel over the course of the option. Would a cap have much value to the airline if the strike price were $1000 instead? That means the airline will pay market price all the way up to $1000. That doesn't sound like a very interesting hedge. The airline would not pay very much for that kind of hedge. An option with a strike price far away from the market price and not worth exercising is called an out-of-the-money option. The farther out-of-the-money an option is (the higher the strike price for a call, for example), the cheaper it will be.

It is possible to sell a call with a strike price below the market. If a trader buys a $60 call on physical crude oil when the market is at $66, he can exercise the option immediately and make $6, so obviously the option is worth at least $6 to the trader. This is called an In the Money option. The deeper an option is in the money, the more expensive it will be. The same logic applies to puts, of course. Try to work out examples of Out of the Money and In the Money puts yourselves.

Options can be a great way to hedge but they cost money to buy. The premium depends on the underlying (volatility), the tenor (how long the option lasts), the strike price (exercise price of the option), and the market level when the deal is done. For those of you who are curious about seeing how option prices move as you adjust these inputs, a little searching around the internet should find you some simple option pricers. Most of them are designed for shares (stocks) but the principles are pretty much the same. You can try adjusting volatility, tenor, and strike price, moving each one independently to see how the option premium changes.

11

Hedging and Portfolio Risk

11.1 How do Traders Really Manage Price Risk?

Simple textbook definitions and examples of hedging use single positions and specific hedges. If a trader is long 35,000 mt of Jet fuel which he going to sell using Platts US Gulf Jet Fuel prices for the average of December 2022, he sells 35,000 mt of December 2022 Platts US Gulf Jet swaps. If the trader also has a position in Singapore where he is short 35,000 mt of Jet fuel which he will buy using December 2022 Platts Singapore Jet Fuel (Kero) prices, he buys 35,000 mt of December 2022 Platts Singapore Jet Fuel (Kero) swaps. Each position the trader has is hedged with a specific derivative perfectly aligned with the pricing market and the timing of the pricing. This goes on for each deal in the trader's portfolio (or book). For every individual position, there is a corresponding hedge. Each long position is offset with a specific short hedge. Each short position is offset with a corresponding long hedge. In reality, traders don't work that way.

It is true that most traders hedge their positions. It is usually company policy to hedge. Traders, desks, or regional offices are required to have flat or nearly flat positions. There can be slight imbalances from day-to-day; a trader might be long a few thousand tonnes one day and short a few thousand the next. On average, though, and with no large deviations from zero, the trader is flat. But the company might measure risk at a different level, perhaps by desk or by region. What is a desk? Or a region?

Trading companies are usually organized by trader, desk, region, and global positions. Traders usually specialize in one area of the market. So a trader might be a fuel oil trader who buys and sells cracked fuel oil, straight run fuel oil, fuel oil blending components, and vacuum gasoil. A distillates trader deals with diesel, gasoil, kerosene, and jet fuel. A gasoline trader works with gasoline, naphtha, reformate, butane, ethanol, MMT, etc. And so on up and down the barrel. The bigger the company the more likely it is to have more specialized traders. A big trading company or an oil major might have traders who trade only jet fuel, for example.

It makes sense to group similar traders together. They can exchange information about their specific market and understand how that information affects supply, demand, and prices. They can cover each other in case of one of the traders is unavailable. A gasoline trader knows the value of alkylate and where to market it; a crude oil trader might not even know what alkylate is! So all the gasoline traders sit together in the office, creating one physical "desk" for those grades of oil. All of their positions can be grouped together since all of the products they deal with have closely related prices.

Regional offices are made up of various desks. A large trading company with an office in Singapore might have a crude oil desk, a naphtha desk, a gasoline desk, a jet desk, a gasoil desk, a cracked fuel desk, a feedstocks desk, an LPG (butane and propane) desk, and so on. Each regional office would have a similar group of desks. So a large trading company with five regional offices might have gasoline desks in Singapore, Dubai, Geneva, New York, and Houston. Each desk contributes to the overall position of the office.

At this point senior management in Geneva or London can analyze and manage their risk in a variety of ways. They can break out the positions of each individual trader. They can break out the risk by desk in each office (the positions and hedges of the crude desk in Houston, for example). They can do it by office (or region). They can also look at it globally by product (what is the overall position of all the fuel oil desks combined) or globally by office.

Astute readers might wonder why management would care to break down the risk by desk, by office, or globally by product if each trader has hedged every one of his positions. Indeed, if each trader hedges perfectly then he has no price risk. In that case, each desk has a perfectly flat position. Since each desk is perfectly flat, the office is perfectly flat as well. Management doesn't need to look at the positions except to see how much and with whom the traders are trading. So why would they organize risk by desk, by office, or globally by product (or crude)?

The answer is that traders, desks, offices, and trading companies do not hedge perfectly. I said at the start that traders need to create risk to make money. One of the most fundamental ways to create risk without making it excessive is to hedge imperfectly. I discussed this in the section on Basis Risk. Traders sometimes create basis risk because they have no choice. The only

11 Hedging and Portfolio Risk

hedging instrument available to them is not exactly aligned with their price risk. More often, traders actually want basis risk so they intentionally hedge with a slightly different derivative (slightly different in how the price might move) or with a related but different physical position.

There are many examples of hedging that creates basis risk, but basis risk usually means hedging with a different underlying or hedging with a different timing. In the first case, this could be hedging jet fuel by selling crude oil futures. In the second case, it could be hedging March price risk by selling June swaps. The first case, jet prices versus crude prices, is called a "crack spread." The second case, March prices versus June prices, is called a time spread. So a trader who is long a prompt cargo of 250,000 bbl of jet fuel which will be sold using June Platts prices can satisfy the rule that he must hedge his positions by selling 250 lots of December Brent crude oil futures. Overall he is balanced: long 250,000 bbl of jet and short 250,000 bbl of crude oil futures. The zero at the bottom of the spreadsheet satisfies his management. If they choose to dig into his position, they will see that while he is flat, he has created a crack spread and a time spread.

If the traders on a desk are pooling their P + L, they can use each other's positions as hedges. If one trader on the distillate desk is long 30,000 mt of diesel in-tank in Singapore, this could be partially hedged by another trader's fixed price sale of 25,000 mt of gasoil to an importer in the Philippines. The balance of 5000 mt of length might then be hedged by selling a swap. Another trader on the distillate desk might decide he wants to buy 500,000 bbl of July Singapore diesel swaps and sell July ICE gasoil futures against that. The head of the desk might take a position on the time spreads in the Singapore market and sell 500,000 bbl of swaps for July 2022 and buy 500,000 bbl of swaps for Dec 2022. All of these positions leave the desk flat overall while creating basis risks. Some of the trades move the risk around. In this example, the trader who bought Singapore diesel swaps and sold ICE gasoil futures sees that position in his book but senior management looking at the overall risk would see that the desk was now short 500,000 bbl of July ICE gasoil futures and long 500,000 bbl of Dec swaps (in addition to the other physical positions I mentioned).

Each desk in the office will operate in the same way. The gasoline desk might be long NY Harbor barge prices and short Singapore prices. The crude desk might be long August Dubai and short December Murban. And so on for each desk. Senior management can look at each desk's overall position individually or they can combine all the positions to see what the office's overall position looks like. In this case, they would convert everything to barrels (as if the risk were all in crude oil, typically as if the position were in Brent or WTI). The office would still be flat, but management could see the basis risk. Singapore might be long time spreads (long prompt prices and short forward prices) or have an arbitrage risk (long prices in Singapore and short prices in the West). If management doesn't agree with a position or think it creates too much risk, they can ask the traders to reduce that risk or simply take an opposite position on their own.

All of this balancing and offsetting of risk from the level of the individual trader's book to the global positions by product or by office means that traders don't generally hedge specific cargoes with perfect hedges. When a cargo is being priced in (i.e., the position is getting long as the prices become known), the risk could be offset by another position which is pricing out at the same time. Any imbalances might be hedged with the most liquid derivative, crude oil futures. Alternatively, if a trader is getting long a physical cargo in Asia, he might hedge the risk by selling swaps in the US Gulf Coast if he wants to be long prices in the East and short prices in the West. If a trader has only one position, one cargo, at a time, then it is easy to point to his physical risk and the derivative and figure out how the cargo was hedged, even if it had been hedged with intentional basis risk. But what if the trader has many positions on physical, swaps, futures, and options? If five traders are all working together on a shared book, then there would likely be many different short and long positions across the globe and the calendar. The head of the desk might hedge daily imbalances by buying and selling crude oil futures without concern for basis risk. The desk will be flat at the end of the day but it might be long physical diesel fuel in Singapore, a bit short diesel fuel in Europe and short WTI futures to bring the position to flat. It would be hard to point to any specific trade and say it was a hedge against a specific cargo.

As part of my work as an expert witness in trading disputes, I am often asked to evaluate hedges or hypothetical hedges. Hedging is a new concept for the legal profession. I don't know of any judges who have a background in trading. Arbitrators typically have more industry experience, but probably not as traders. There is, for now, no set principle for including or excluding hedging losses and gains (or hypothetical losses and gains) from a claim or lawsuit. It is likely that if it can be demonstrated that a hedge was put on specifically against a physical position, then that hedge would be taken into account by the court or arbitration tribunal. Still, that is not certain in all cases; the jurisprudence is mixed, though the general shift is toward accepting hedging where it occurs.

This becomes tricky when the trader or company uses portfolio hedging, as most do. English law is concerned with two principles in assessing damages: causation and remoteness. Causation means there must a clear link between the physical trade and the hedge (derivatives or other). Did the physical breach of contract cause losses or gains on the purported hedge? Can the specific hedges be pointed out in the trader's book?

Remoteness deals with foreseeability; are the losses or gains in hedging a natural part of the way business is done? Some traders might not hedge as a matter of course either because they choose not to or because they are unable to hedge. Some small traders have not signed ISDAs or don't have access to futures exchanges to hedge with futures or to clear swaps. It is a given, however, that when deals between major oil companies or between large trading companies are concluded hedging will take place.

For a deeper insight into court decisions on hedging and how judges and arbitrators use remoteness and causation, I recommend "A Practical Guide to Hedging: Should You Hedge or Already Be Hedged When Your Counterparty Defaults" by Damian Honey and Michael Buffham of HFW.

I have been involved in a few cases which involved hedging and hypothetical hedging. In one case, a buyer refused to accept delivery of a cargo which was sold later into a falling market. The buyer tried to argue that the seller should have, could have and probably did hedge the cargo. There was no evidence of any hedging but the buyer argued that "everyone hedges" and therefore the seller should have hedged. Had the seller hedged, the claim would have been significantly reduced. I was able to demonstrate that the seller did not hedge and could not hedge because he did not have access to derivative markets. The seller was a small trader so this was plausible and true. It was clear that it was not foreseeable that the seller would hedge (remoteness) and therefore it was not acceptable to consider hypothetical hedges.

In another case, the claimant was a large trading company who ran their trading book on a portfolio basis. A cargo of jet fuel was delayed during delivery and sold later at a much lower market. The trader claimed losses from the price drop. The other side insisted that "everyone hedges," especially a large trading company, and therefore the losses should be offset by the gain from hedges. The trader turned over his daily position reports for nearly a year of trading as well as the daily deal confirmation of all futures and swaps traded during the period. It was clear that the daily positions of a very, very large portfolio of physical and derivative trades (trades extending from prompt to three years out and across the globe including WTI, Heating Oil, Brent, ICE LS Gasoil, and swaps for various products in New York, Europe, and Singapore) were generally close to zero. That is to say, the traders ran a nearly flat book (it might have been as much as 150,000 bbl long or short on rare occasions but was on average very close to flat). So were the traders hedged or not? That was the question put to the court.

The other side (the ones being asked to pay for the losses on the cargo) insisted that the trader was hedged. "Look at the book," they said. "It's almost always flat. They were hedged." They insisted that the traders point out the exact hedges to the court, claiming the traders were hiding it and refusing to show it. I explained to the court that the traders ran a portfolio composed of dozens if not hundreds of positions which generally created an overall flat book, but that there were no specific hedges in the portfolio. The trader might have been long that jet fuel position against a short position in gasoline in New York or gasoil in Rotterdam. The trader might have been overall short jet fuel prices in the market in question during some periods of time over the year while being long Brent crude oil futures one year forward during those periods. The portfolio might have been long millions of barrels of prompt oil and short two years forward at other times. It was impossible to point out a specific hedge of the jet cargo for the simple reason that the trader did not put on a hedge specific to that cargo! The court agreed; "portfolio hedging" is too remote to find a direct link (causation) between losses on a specific physical cargo and gains on derivatives. A flat (neither long nor short) portfolio is not necessarily a hedged portfolio.

It is important to bear in mind that just because a trader, a desk, or an entire trading company has a flat book doesn't mean that losses are impossible. Traders have lost millions running hedged books. A large trading company lost a few billion dollars buying gasoline and selling heating oil on the NYMEX a few decades ago. The position was balanced (flat), but gasoline went down while heating oil went up. The position was huge and led to massive losses. Another trader I knew took large positions on the difference in price (spread) between high sulfur and low sulfur fuel oil in the same market. He bought swaps on low sulphur fuel and sold swaps on high sulphur fuel for the same quantity, in the same market and over the same period. His book was flat. Was he hedged? He lost over $100 million on that trade, so I guess not.

Of course, if you can lose hundreds of millions trading a flat book, you should be able to make hundreds of millions, if not billions, trading a flat book. And that is what traders do! Traders create risk in order to make money. That is the premise we started with; no risk, no reward. But for the most part, traders run flat books. They buy and sell different things at the same time. They use their market knowledge and experience to anticipate, predict and sometimes assist market movements in time spreads, cracks, arbitrages, and inter-product spreads and make millions. They buy millions of barrels, put them in storage, hedge the risk, and make billions, like they did during the Super Contango caused by COVID. And they do all that with flat books.

12

Conclusion

My motivations to write this book came both from being confined during COVID and my teaching experience. Most new hires know next to nothing about risk, oil trading, and hedging when they join a company. Most senior managers in banks and oil companies know little about what their traders do on a day-to-day basis. Many people in the market who use derivatives and futures don't really understand them. I hope this book has helped those kinds of people gain at least some understanding of risk and risk management in oil markets. I intentionally avoided formulas and calculations to keep the book accessible. To be honest, most oil traders don't need to know anything more than addition and multiplication. There is little complicated math that applies to physical oil trading, futures, forwards, and swaps. Options are a different story, which is why this book covers them in a particular way.

Risk is at the heart of oil trading. It has defined the heroes and goats of the industry since the first drops of crude oil were pumped out of the ground. Traders seek and create risk in order to make money. Each trader and each company in the industry has to decide how much and what kinds of risk he is willing to take. I have outlined the principles of how to manage some of those risks and hope that my explanations are clear and simple enough to be understood. I hope that my readers choose to become honest, moral oil traders and apply the advice and recommendations I provided. Above all, I hope that their trading careers are profitable in every sense.

Nice, March 2023

Appendices

Glossary

Arbitrage

A situation where the price of the same oil is different in two markets and typically a profit can be made by shipping the oil from the cheaper to the more expensive market. When a product habitually flows from one market to another, traders talk about the arbitrage being "open" (the oil can be bought in one market and shipped/sold in the other and earn a profit) or being "closed" (the difference in price between the two markets is too small to earn a profit by moving the oil from one to the other). Often, an arbitrage is open or closed depending on the cost of shipping (freight costs to move from cheap market to the higher priced one).

Argus

Argus Media is a price reporting agency that publishes market prices for crude oil and oil products. See also Platts.

At-the-Money

An option whose strike price is the same as the underlying market price for the commodity. When the price of crude oil is $80, an At-the-Money call has a strike price of $80.

Asian Option or Average Price Option

An option which settles (pays out) against an average of prices over a period of time. This common hedging derivative can also be understood as "half a swap," meaning the good half which pays you money while letting you ignore the bad half which makes you pay out.

Backwardation

A type of market price structure where the prices for prompt delivery are higher than the prices for deliveries made later. E.g., the price for September Gasoil futures is $900 while the price for October Gasoil futures is $850. September is in backwardation with respect to October. The market is "backwardated" or it is a "backwardated market."

BFOE or BFOET

Brent, Forties, Oseberg, Ekofisk, Troll. These are the crudes that make up the deliverable qualities under the Brent Forward Contract for North Sea Crude. Platts uses "BFOE" while many traders and others use BFOE; they mean the same thing. Shortly, Platts and the market will integrate Midland West Texas Intermediate into the Brent Forward market. It is likely that Platts will continue to use BFOE as their abbreviation and the others will continue to use BFOET.

BFOE or BFOET can also refer to the Forward contract itself (see Brent Forward).

Brent Forward Contract

A forward contract for delivery of one of five North Sea crude oils (see BFOE). Also called "Paper Brent" and "30 Day Brent" contracts.

Call Option

An option which allows the buyer of the option to purchase the underlying asset at the pre-agreed price if he exercises the option. The buyer of a call can quite literally call you up and make you sell to him at the price you agreed to when you entered into the option contract no matter where the market price is today.

CFR

Cost and Freight, an Incoterm which means the seller will deliver the cargo to the buyer. The price includes the cost of the cargo and shipping but not insurance. Risk passes from the seller to the buyer when the cargo is put on board at the load port.

CIF

Cost, Insurance, and Freight which is an Incoterm. Pronounced "See, Eye, Eff" or "siff." The seller will deliver the cargo to the buyer. In addition to the terms and conditions of CFR (see above) the seller will arrange and pay for insurance for the cargo during shipment (covering loss and contamination essentially).

Clearing House

The corporation or entity that is the counterparty to all trades on an exchange. When you buy Brent futures, you are trading against ICE, not against Vitol, Shell, Adnoc, or whoever else happened to be selling at the moment you bought.

Cleared Swap

Swaps are usually OTC contracts, but counterparty risk and banking regulations led market participants to move swap trading to regulated exchanges like ICE and CME NYMEX (the clearing exchanges have slightly different names). Two traders conclude a swap between themselves and decide to "clear" it. The contract is broken and the exchange becomes the new counterparty for both the buyer and seller. This eliminates counterparty risk and greatly reduces margining requirements under international banking rules. Today many liquid swaps can be traded directly on the exchange trading platform without ever being OTC.

Contango

A type of market price structure where the prices for prompt delivery are lower than the prices for deliveries made later. E.g., the price for September WTI futures is $80 while the price for October WTI futures is $85. October is in contango with respect to September. The market is "in contango" or it is a "contango market."

Cracking

A refining process which takes big hydrocarbons (oil molecules) and breaks them into smaller, more valuable molecules. For example, a cracking unit might take fuel oil and "crack" the molecules into hydrocarbons with 7 or 8 carbon atoms; it has turned heavy fuel into gasoline.

Crack Spread

The difference in price between crude oil and an oil product measured in dollars per barrel. If crude oil is at $80 per barrel and diesel is at $100, the crack spread for diesel is $20 per barrel. This is a positive crack spread. Crack spreads for heavy fuel oil can be negative which means turning crude oil into fuel oil is a money-losing activity. If we add up weighted average crack spreads for all the products a refinery makes, we get the refining margin (see Refining Margin).

Crude Oil

A dark, viscous liquid made up of dozens or even hundreds of molecules called hydrocarbons (composed principally of carbon and hydrogen). It is naturally occurring, typically found deep in the earth's crust and non-renewable. It has limited direct uses and must be refined into oil products such as diesel fuel, jet fuel, and gasoline.

DAP

Delivered At Place is an Incoterm in which the seller will deliver the product to practically any named place or point. The risk is passed from the seller to the buyer at the place named in the contract. DAP has replaced the previous Incoterm DES (Delivered Ex-Ship). Many buyers like to use DAP (or previously DES) with transfer of risk in their own tanks after discharge since it meant they had transit losses or pollution risk. Exxon, with its painful memory of the Exxon Valdez, has always preferred buying DES and now DAP.

Derivative

A derivative is a financial contract whose price is derived from the underlying physical market. It is called a "financial" contract because there is no physical delivery of oil, only a payment of cash. If I bet you $1000 that oil prices will be over $90 next week, that is a derivative. The settlement of the bet is determined by the price of the underlying, which is to say oil. If the market next week is $120, you pay me the $1000. If the market is under $90, I pay you $1000. No physical oil is exchanged. Futures contracts are not derivatives because they can lead to physical delivery, but they are mostly used as if they were derivatives (i.e., not used to make or take physical delivery).

EFP or Exchange of Futures for Physicals

A contract which swaps a physical position for a futures position. I sell you my cargo of gasoil and you sell me the equivalent amount of ICE gasoil futures.

Fixed Price

A price which has been set and is known. If you agree to buy a cargo of naphtha at $700 per metric tonne, that is a fixed price deal. By definition, futures and forwards are fixed price deals. Brent futures are bought and sold at $92.35 per barrel, for example. Swaps are also fixed price contracts. A fixed price in a deal creates a position, meaning it makes the trader either long or short.

Floating Price

A contract price which has not been determined or fixed. The price will be determined later but is for now going up and down with the market; it is floating up and down. A floating price contract will normally stipulate that the price will be set using market prices at some point or average over time in the future. PRA's like Platts and Argus are the most common source for discovering and applying the market price to a floating price contract. A floating price might be Platts Monthly Average for Jet Fuel Cargoes FOB Northwest Europe during the calendar month of next October. We don't know what the market price will be during next October; it might go up or down. The contract price will be set by using the prices reported by Platts during the month of October; the floating price becomes a fixed price as it is reported.

FOB

Free On Board. This in an Incoterm (International Commercial Term) which means the seller makes the oil available in a port, the buyer has to find a vessel and load the oil onto his vessel. Risk (contamination and losses) passes from the seller to the buyer once the oil touches the vessel (usually defined as the vessel's permanent manifold).

Forward Contract

A fixed price contract for delivery of oil in the future. A forward is different from a futures contract in that it is not traded through an exchange (and is therefore called OTC or "over the counter") and is based on delivery of a full cargo lot. A Brent Forward for December means a fixed price deal for 600,000 barrels of one of the crudes in BFOET (see above) during the calendar month of December. Forward markets in Brent and Dubai are still essential parts of the market. Most other forward markets have disappeared and been replaced with futures and swaps.

Forward Curve

A plot of prices for the delivery of a commodity at different times in the future. A futures exchange typically lists contracts by month (which we call the "tenor"). If we take a snapshot of the prices for futures contracts, plot them on a graph and draw a line, we construct the forward curve. The forward curve does not predict prices; it shows prices right now for different delivery timing.

Front-line Contract or Front-line Futures

The first contract listed on a futures exchange. Exchanges list futures contracts by tenor (month of delivery) with the soonest listed first and followed by the later delivery contracts in calendar order (Jan, Feb, Mar, Apr, etc.). Front-line contract tenors may be different from exchange to exchange as well as for different commodities. So, on the 2nd of October, front-line ICE Brent is December while front-line ICE Gas Oil is October and front-line NYMEX WTI is November because they all expire on different dates.

Futures or Futures Contracts

A contract to buy or sell oil for delivery in the future. The contract is concluded on an exchange, at a fixed price and with invariably standard terms and conditions. If you buy one December 2028 WTI futures contract today at $85 per barrel and hold onto that contract until expiry, you will receive 1000 barrels of WTI crude oil at Cushing, Oklahoma during the month of December. You will pay $85 for that oil whatever the market price is at the time (and I am confident it will not be $85).

Hedge or Hedging

An equal and opposite position on a derivative or even a different physical position which offsets losses caused by price movements. If a trader is long, he hedges by selling a derivative such as a futures contract. And vice versa. Hedging prevents losses but also prevents further gains; a perfect hedge should lock in the financial result of the overall position (physical plus derivative).

ICE

Intercontinental Exchange, the futures exchange that replaced the IPE and moved oil Brent and Gas Oil futures onto a purely electronic platform. The name is pronounced the same way as ice (frozen water). Saying "Eye, See, Eee" is a sure sign you are an outsider or neophyte.

Incoterms

Incoterms is an acronym for International Commercial Terms which are published by the International Chamber of Commerce. In oil trading we use FOB, CFR, CIF, and DAP. These abbreviations cover the risks and responsibilities of the buyer and the seller in international transactions. It is possible and not uncommon to have a commercial contract whose GT&Cs are Incoterms (i.e., "All other terms and conditions as per Incoterms latest edition."). The key feature for most people is the transfer of risk. For example, FOB, CFR, and CIF all pass the risk from the seller to the buyer as soon as the oil is loaded at the port of origin.

Kb or kbbl

Kilo-barrels or 1000 barrels. Nobody says "kilo-barrels," so if you see 50 kb, 50 kbbl, or even 50k bbl, read it as Fifty Thousand Barrels. The "b" is obvious, but the origin of "bbl" is disputed. One story says it comes from "blue barrels" because of better quality oil being delivered in barrels painted blue but this tale appears untrue. In any case, one US barrel is 42 US gallons or 159 liters.

Long or Long Position

Physically, owning oil or the right to oil. For price risk, it means buying oil or a derivative at a fixed price. Being long the price of oil means you make money when the market goes up and lose money when it goes down.

Margin or Margining

Counterparties to a trade that has price risk (e.g., a futures contract or a swap) might ask for collateral in the form of cash or highly liquid assets like gold. When a futures contract is bought, it is not necessary to pay for the entire value of the underlying. If you buy one lot of WTI at $80, it is notionally worth $80,000. But you will be unlikely to take physical delivery or if you do it won't be for some time (in the future). The exchange is worried that the position will lose money. If the market drops to $75, NYMEX worries that you might run away to avoid the $5000 loss (one lot = 1000 barrels; you bought 1000 barrels at $80 but they are now worth only $75). NYMEX will require a security deposit for each lot you buy. This might be $8000 or $8 per barrel for WTI. This security deposit is called a margin.

Margin Call

If your position on an exchange is losing money (if you closed your positions you would have a loss), the exchange will ask you to top up your margin to get it back to the required amount per lot. If the margin requirement is $8000 per lot, you bought one lot at $80 and the market is at $79, you must send the exchange a top-up payment of $1000 by the close of the day or they will close out your position.

NYMEX or CME NYMEX

New York Mercantile Exchange is the exchange where WTI futures are traded. NYMEX was bought by the Chicago Mercantile Exchange (CME) in 2008. CME NYMEX also trades gasoline futures (RBOB) and heating oil futures.

Option

A contract that gives the buyer the right but not the obligation to do something. For commodities, options give the buyer the right to buy or sell an underlying commodity at a pre-agreed price. If you book a reception hall for a wedding, you might have to pay a non-refundable deposit which you lose if the groom runs off to Peru. If the groom is steadfast, you have a party and pay the amount you agreed when paid the deposit. That is an example of a call option with you as the buyer. You don't have to throw a wedding party, but the hotel has a commitment and must give you the room if you call and ask for it.

OTC or Over the Counter

A financial contract or derivative which is not traded on a futures exchange. Most oil swaps were OTC until the Financial Crisis of 2007-2009. Now most oil swaps are "cleared" through an exchange which makes them behave and get regulated like futures contracts.

Platts

Platts is the generic name for a variety of publications from S&P Global which include crude oil reports, oil products reports, and shipping market reports. Platts is a Price Reporting Agency which is used for most floating price deals that use PRA prices. If you are buying or selling a cargo of diesel fuel anywhere in the world using "floating" prices, you are probably using Platts.

Put Option

An option which allows the buyer of the option to sell the underlying asset at the pre-agreed price if he exercises the option. The buyer of a put can quite literally call you up and make you buy from him at the price you agreed to when you entered into the option contract no matter where the market price is today.

Refining Margin

The gross or net profit in dollars per barrel a refiner makes by buying crude and turning into products (e.g. gasoline and diesel). Crude is the input; products are the output. The price of the crude is simple; it is the cost per barrel in the market. The price of the products has to be converted into $/bbl. Each individual calculation (Price of Gasoil minus Price of Crude Oil) is called a crack spread. A refinery produces many products so each crack spread has a different weighting in the profitability. Adding up the weighted averages of the crack spreads gives us the refining margin. Each refinery has its own margin at any given time. Analysts and traders use standard models and the main market reference prices to calculate a notional refining margin (on a gross basis). This might use Platts Dated Brent for the crude price and Platts Diesel, Jet, Gasoline, and Fuel Oil Barge prices for the products, for example.

Short or Short Position

Physically, having an obligation to deliver oil to somebody. From a price point of view, it means selling oil at a fixed price when you either don't have that oil or if you don't yet know how much you will have to pay for the oil you just sold. It is uncommon to have short positions in everyday life.

Spot or Spot Deal or Spot Delivery

Usually the earliest delivery dates traded in the market. "Spotness" depends on the underlying and the geographical market. Spot barge deals in Rotterdam can be for delivery in 3–12 days from the deal date. Spot crude deals in West Africa are typically for delivery in 30–45 days from the deal date. Spot futures denote the "front-line" contract on the exchange which is the tenor with the earliest delivery.

Swap

A financial contract or derivative which turns a fixed price into a floating price or vice versa. In simple terms it's a "bet" on where the market will be over some period in the future, typically over a calendar month. The buyer and seller of the swap set the "starting price" (the fixed price of the swap) of the bet and then agree on how to see if the market was high or lower than the starting price. Common oil swaps use Platts to measure the market. If you buy a Platts Dated Brent Swap for October at $90, you will make money if Platts reports the average price of Dated Brent during October is higher than

$90. That is the same as betting someone Platts Dated Brent will be higher than $90 in October, but we call that a "swap" because that sounds more professional.

Bibliography

This bibliography does not list only the material I have referred to in my own writing or used as background research but also lists books and sources that I recommend in general for learning about the oil market.

Bower, T., 2009, *The Squeeze: Oil, Money and Greed in the 21st Century*, HarperCollins.

BP Oil International, *General Terms and Conditions for the Sale and Purchase of Oil and Oil Products*.

Downey, M., 2009, *Oil 101*, Wooden Table Press.

Fatouh, B., March 2012, *The Dubai Benchmark and Its Role in the International Oil Pricing System*, OIES.

Fatouh, B. et al., May 2018, *Quarterly Forum Issue 113*, Oxford Institute for Energy Studies.

Honey, D. and Buffham, M., July 2018 Commodities, *A Practical Guide to Hedging: Should You Hedge or Already Be Hedged When Your Counterparty Defaults?*, HFW.

Imsirovic, A., 2021, *Trading and Price Discovery for Crude Oils: Growth and Development of International Oil Markets*, Palgrave Macmillan.

Imsirovic, A. and Chapman, K., Oxford Institute for Energy Studies comments and articles.

———, July 2022, *The Brent Benchmark - Where Do We Stand?*.

———, March 2022, *The Future of the Brent Oil Benchmarch, A Radical Makeover*.

Schofield, N., 2007, *Commodity Derivatives: Markets and Applications*, John Wiley and Sons.

Taleb, N., 2008, *The Black Swan*, Random House.

Index

A

Agarkov, Dimitry
　Tinkoff Credit Systems, credit card contract 12
American law
　US law, US courts 28
Arbitrage price risk
　basis risk example using diesel arbitrage pricing 89
Arbitration
　court, costs of dispute 31
Argus
　price reporting agencies (PRA), market prices, floating prices 59, 71
Aron, J.
　compliance, trade entry, book-keeping 38
Average Price Options (APO)
　Asian call options, Caps 137

B

Back-to-back deals
　definition of 3
　example of 3
Backwardation
　as a market indicator, bullish indicator 129
　convenience yield 125
　graph of backwardation, forward curve in backwardation 128
　market structure, elephants and bottles of water 123
Barings Bank
　Nick Leeson, example of derivative risk 25
Basic Rule and Deviation
　breach of contract, accepting 13, 15
Basis risk
　crack spread, crude price *vs.* product price 145
　definition and examples of 85
　imperfect hedge, spread risk 84
Basis risk hedging
　example using crude oil pricing 87
Bill of lading pricing

Index

B/L pricing, around B/L floating price 67
Block chain
   letters of credit, e-documents, Komgo, Trakk 43
Bower, Tom
   The Squeeze, great oil traders, short squeeze, John Deuss, Transworld Oil 41
Breach of contract
   trading dispute, court case 31
Brent-Dubai swap/swap trade
   swap spread trade 108
Brent futures
   ICE Brent, North Sea oil futures 113
Brent *vs.* Dubai spread risk
   crude oil arbitrage, crude price hedging 104
Burry, Michael
   The Big Short, bleeding losses, home-run hitters 50

C

Caps
   Asian call options, Average Price Options (APO) 137
Causation, in hedging
   hedging in legal disputes, applying hedging to claims 146
Chicago Mercantile Exchange (CME)
   New York Mercantile Exchange (NYMEX), WTI futures 114
China Aviation Oil
   derivative risk, example of 24
Cleared swaps
   clearing, exchange-traded swaps 101
Clearing House
   futures exchange, exchange, counterparty for futures 113

Collusion
   collusion *vs.* cooperation 40
Commercial Court in London
   English High Court 31
Completion of Discharge (COD) pricing 60
Compliance
   J. Aron and trade entry errors 38
   zero tolerance 38
Compliance department
   Middle Office 35
Contango
   as a market indicator, bearish indicator 130
   graph of contango, forward curve in contango 126
   market structure, elephants and bottles of water 123
Contracts
   binding contracts, boiler plate, standard wording 12
Contractual risk
   contracts, legal risk 12
   contracts, need of 27
   English Law, governing law, jurisdiction 28
   value of good operators 27
Convenience yield
   backwardation, economist's explanation 125
Cost, Insurance, Freight (CIF) Incoterm 11
Crack spread
   crude price *vs.* product price, basis risk, spread risk 145

D

Derivatives
   basic derivatives 95
   futures contract, futures, futures exchange 113
   swaps 95
Deuss, John

short squeeze, Transworld Oil,
  The Squeeze 41
Transworld Oil, Brent squeeze,
  short squeeze 41

E

English High Court
  Commercial Court in London 31
English Law
  preferred law 28
Expiry of futures contracts
  physical delivery, last trading day,
    settlement of futures 115

F

Faroffistan
  floating price, corruption, market
    moves 66
Flat
  neutral, no price risk 62
Floating price
  average day pricing, five day
    pricing example 73
  bill of lading pricing, B/L pricing,
    around B/L 67
  floating formula, Platts-related 59
  moving the market, market
    manipulation, moving Platts
    prices 68
  notice of readiness (NOR) 67
  Platts Window, Platts MOC, the
    Window 68
  price risk on average pricing,
    price risk and hedging risk 74
Floating price formula
  example of floating price clause
    71
  example of floating price deal,
    COD pricing 60
  Mean of Platts 71
Floor

Asian put, producer option,
  average price put option 138
Force Majeure 4
  BP's Force Majeure clauses,
    definition of 30
  definition of 10
Forward contracts
  standardized contracts, liquid
    instruments 132
Forward curve
  graph of backwardation, curve in
    backwardation 128
  graph of contango, forward curve
    in contango 127
  market, structure, shape of the
    curve, futures curve 126
Free on Board (FOB)
  Incoterm (International
    Commercial Term) 8
Futures contracts
  Brent futures, ICE Brent 113
  definition, main elements 116
  expiry, last trading day, settlement
    of futures 115
  futures, lots, exchange-traded
    futures 113
  tenor, delivery period, contract
    name 115
Futures exchanges
  cleared swaps, clearing,
    exchange-traded swaps 101
Futures prices
  creating 121

G

General Terms and Conditions
  (GT&C's) 29

H

Half a swap

hedging with options, Average Price Options, Asian options 136
Hall, Andy
  price risk, predicting oil prices, Phibro 52
Hedge
  definition of hedge, offsetting loss 79
Hedging
  with options 136
Hedging price risk
  basic principles of 80
  basis risk example using crude oil pricing 87
  basis risk example using diesel pricing 89
  basis risk, imperfect hedge 84
  example using crude oil pricing 87
  hedging using physical cargoes, offsetting positions 84
  hedging with futures, using futures to hedge 117
  locking in profits, locking in losses, loss avoidance 83
  portfolio hedging, portfolio risk, basis risk trading 143, 144
  swaps *vs.* futures 119
Hedging with futures
  manual hedging, daily hedging 120
  using futures to hedge, WTI and US crude 117
Hin Leong trading
  letters of credit, trading scandal, fraud 43

ICE Futures Abu Dhabi (IFAD)
  Murban futures 121
Imsirovic, Adi

Trading and Price Discovery for Crude Oils, history of oil pricing 132
  value of good operators, *Trading and Price Discovery for Crude Oil* 26
Incoterm (International Commercial Term)
  FOB, CIF, CFR, DDP, etc. 8

Jurisdiction
  court, arbitration 31

K

Kahneman, Daniel
  Thinking Fast and Slow, trading biases 84
Know Your Client (KYC)
  compliance, finance 35

L

Leeson, Nick
  Barings Bank, Singapore, bank fraud, prison 19
Legal risk
  cheating, stealing 33
  cooperation *vs.* collusion 40
  facilitating payments, bribery, bribes 39
  illegal trading, consequence of 17
  in trading 16
  lying, bribery, market manipulation 16
  managing 32
  Middle Office, compliance department 35
  moral issues, spinning the market, lying 32
  trading scandals, bribery 34
Letters of credit

digital letters of credit, block
 chain, documents 43
 payment guaranty 43
Long positions
 long as a physical notion 53
Long price positions
 Frowny Face, losing money,
  adverse market move 56
 long, being long, going long,
  fixed price purchase risk 54
 Smiley Face 54
Loss avoidance
 hedging, trading bias 84
Loss limits, setting 51

M

Magoon, Joseph
 Squire, Patton, Boggs; lawyer,
  English law, US law 28
Managing risk
 in trading 23
Market manipulation
 Glencore, collusion, Platts MOC
  manipulation 41
 moving the market, market
  manipulation, moving Platts
  prices 68
 short squeeze 41
Market on Close
 Platts Window, Platts MOC, the
  Window 68
Market structure
 contango and backwardation,
  elephants and bottles of water
  123
 forward curve, shape of the curve,
  futures curve 126
Market structure and price
 prediction
 supply and demand, bullish or
  bearish 129
Mean of Platts

market reference price, average of
 high and low price 71
Middle Office
 compliance department 35
*Misbehaving: The Making of
 Behavioral Economics*
 Richard Thaler, trading biases,
  psychology 84
Montepeque, Jorge
 Platts, Brent market, Platts
  Window 41
Murban futures
 ICE Futures Abu Dhabi (IFAD)
  121

N

New York Mercantile Exchange
 (NYMEX)
 Chicago Mercantile Exchange
  (CME) 114
Notice of Readiness (NOR)
 arrival at port 67

O

Offsetting risk
 hedging using physical cargoes,
  offsetting positions 84
Operational risk
 cargo losses 10
 contaminations and quality
  problems 10
 delivery delays 10
 derivative operations 24
 examples of 5
 Force Majeure, Acts of God 11
 managing risk, back office systems
  25
 operations, things go wrong 23
 spreadsheets, back office systems,
  reporting 24
 value of good operators,
  professional operations 26

Options
  calls and puts, vanilla options 134
  definition of 133
  everyday options, options in regular life 133
  hedging with 136
  option pricing, Black-Scholes, option premiums 139
  selling options, unlimited losses, writing options 139
  volatility, price movements, Vol 140
Option trading
  Floor, Asian put, producer option 138
Option writer
  selling options, unlimited losses, writing options 139

P

Payment risk 17
  definition of 18
  letters of credit, payment guaranty 43
  managing 42
  payment delay, late payment 18
Personal risk
  burn out 20
  in trading 19
  managing 45
  money and happiness, buying happiness 21
  trading and stress 19
Platts
  price reporting agencies (PRA), market prices, floating prices 59
Platts Window
  Platts MOC, the Window 68
Position limits
  example of VAR, compliance issues 36
Predicting prices
  futures and price predictions 121
Price Majeure
  Force Majeure clause, poor use of 30
Price positions
  flat, neutral, no price risk 62
  floating price, floating formula 59
Price reporting agencies (PRA)
  Platts, Argus 59
Price risk
  consumer 65
  definition of 51, 52
  managing 49
  predicting oil prices, Phibro 53
  refiner, refining margins, term contracts 64

R

Reference prices
  illiquid, unclear price references, alternative pricing 99
Remoteness, in hedging
  hedging in legal disputes, applying hedging to claims 146
Risk
  definition of 3

S

Schofield, Neil
  Commodity Derivatives (Wiley Finance, 2007) 36
Short positions
  short as a physical notion 53
Short price positions
  going short in everyday life 57
  short, shorting, going short, being short 57
Short squeeze
  cornering the market, Transworld Oil, John Deuss, Sempra 41
Smiley Face

long, being long, going long,
fixed price purchase risk 54
Spread trade
Brent-Dubai swap/swap, swap
spread trade 108
Stress
in trading, managing 45
Strike price
options, exercising options 141
Swap(s)
definition of 1
derivative 95
example of a swap, MOPS Kero
swap, Singapore jet swap 96
forward curve for swaps, swap
structure 130
imperfect swap hedge, pricing
delays, misalignment of hedge
102
Over the Counter (OTC),
counterparty risk, reporting
101
Platts Arab Gulf prices, illiquid
reference prices 98
unreliable, illiquid reference
prices, Caltex Bahrain Posted
Price 98

Taleb, Nassim
The Black Swan 9
Thaler, Richard
*Misbehaving: The Making of
Behavioral Economics*, trading
biases, psychology 84

The Big Short (Michael Burry) 50
The Black Swan (Nassim Taleb) 49
Thinking Fast and Slow
Daniel Kahneman, biases, trading
psychology 84
*Trading and Price Discovery for Crude
Oils* (Imsirovic, Adi) 132
Trading guru
trading psychologist, therapy 47
Trading plan, setting up 51
Trading styles
nest-builders, home-run hitters,
building P&L 50
Transworld Oil
short squeeze, John Deuss, Brent
squeeze 41

Uniform Commercial Code
US law, US state law 28

Value-At-Risk (VAR)
loss limit 35
Vanilla options
basic options, standard options,
plain options 134
Violation Tracker
anti-corruption, fines, penalties
34
Volatility
option volatility, price
movements, Vol 140